Your Name Means Everything

Strength and Dignity

What the Bible Says to Young Women

About Character, Wisdom, and Faith

Paul & Pam Hainline

NobleMind Press

Your Name Means Everything: Strength and Dignity

Copyright © 2026 Paul & Pam Hainline
All rights reserved.

Published by NobleMind Press
noblemind.study

ISBN 979-8-9954288-2-4 (paperback)
ISBN 979-8-9954288-3-1 (hardcover)

First Edition

Contents

Nobody Told You This

Nobody told you this was coming.

One day you're sitting in a classroom watching the clock. The next day someone hands you a diploma, takes a picture, and the world steps back and says — "Alright. Your turn."

And just like that, the decisions get real.

Not homework-real. Not who-said-what-about-who-real. Real real. The kind of decisions that follow you. The kind that build something — or tear something down. The kind that, ten years from now, you'll either look back on with quiet confidence or with the ache of I wish someone had told me.

Well. Someone is telling you now.

You have been handed something no generation before you has ever had to carry — a small glowing screen that can reach you any hour of the day or night, that never runs out of content, that is specifically, deliberately, and scientifically engineered to keep you looking at it. The people who built it are brilliant. Their entire business model depends on your attention. And they are very, very good at what they do.

Here is what that screen has cost you, and this isn't said to shame you — it's said because it's true and you deserve to know it:

It has trained you to compare yourself to images that aren't real. It has filled your head with voices that don't know you and don't love you. It has made you feel like you're never pretty enough, thin enough, popular enough, interesting enough — never enough

— while feeding you a thousand opinions and very little truth. And it has been doing this since you were old enough to hold it.

That is not your fault. But what you do about it from here — that part is on you.

This book is going to ask something of you that might feel harder than it sounds.

It is going to ask you to slow down.

Not forever. Not dramatically. But long enough to actually think. Long enough to read a passage of Scripture and sit with it instead of scrolling past it. Long enough to ask yourself hard questions and wait for honest answers.

If you can do that — and you can — what you'll find on the other side of that discipline is something the screen has never once been able to give you:

Wisdom.

Not information. Not opinions. Not highlights and hot takes.

Wisdom. The kind that tells you who you really are, how to treat people, what your life is actually for, and how to build something that lasts beyond you.

The only source of that wisdom is God. And He did not leave us without a Word.

This book is built on the Bible. Not on one denomination's interpretation of it. Not on what's popular or comfortable or easy to sell. On the text itself — what it actually says, to whom it was said, and what it means for a young woman standing at the beginning of her life in the twenty-first century.

Some of what you read here will confirm what you already sense is true.

Some of it will challenge what you've been told — or what you've told yourself.

All of it is offered with one purpose: to help you become the woman God designed you to be. Not a perfect woman. Not a woman who never stumbles. But a woman of character. A woman whose word means something. A woman who knows her God, treats people with genuine respect, and understands that the decisions she makes at eighteen, nineteen, and twenty are laying a foundation — for better or worse — that the rest of her life will be built upon.

There is one verse that could serve as the compass for everything that follows. It was written by a man named Solomon — the wisest man who ever lived — and he wrote it near the end of his life, after having tried nearly everything the world had to offer:

> *"The conclusion, when all has been heard, is: fear God and keep His commandments, because this applies to every person."*
> — Ecclesiastes 12:13 (NASB)

Every person. That includes you.

Not when you're older. Not when life settles down. Not after you've figured out who you are. **Now.** At the exact moment you're reading these words.

You don't have to have it all figured out. Nobody does at your age, and anyone who tells you otherwise is either lying or hasn't been tested yet.

But you do have to start.

- Start paying attention to the kind of woman you're becoming.

- Start taking your name seriously.

- Start treating the people around you — especially the young men in your life — the way God says they deserve to be treated.

- Start spending more time with the Book that has the answers and less time with the screen that's selling you lies about your worth.

This book will walk with you through all of it, one chapter at a time. No rush. No shame. Just straight talk from God's Word to a young woman who matters more than she probably knows.

That young woman is you.

Let's get started.

> *"The fear of the Lord is the beginning of wisdom, and the knowledge of the Holy One is understanding."*
> — Proverbs 9:10 (NASB)

CHAPTER 1

Your Name Is Your Most Valuable Asset

Part One: Who You Are

There is something your grandmother's generation understood that yours largely has not been taught.

Your name is not just what people call you.

It is what they think of when they hear it. It is your history walking into the room before you do. It is the invisible record of every promise you kept — and every one you broke. Every time you told the truth when a lie would have been easier. Every time you said something behind someone's back that you wouldn't say to her face. Every time you showed up, and every time you didn't.

Your name is, in the most practical sense, you — the version of you that exists in the minds and memories of everyone who has ever known you.

And right now, at the beginning of your adult life, you are writing the first chapters of what that name will mean.

What God Says About a Name

The wisest man who ever lived — a king named Solomon, who had wealth, power, pleasure, and achievement beyond anything most people can imagine — sat down late in his life and made a simple statement that cuts right through all of it:

> *"A good name is to be more desired than great wealth; favor is better than silver and gold."*
> — Proverbs 22:1 (NASB)

Read that again. He didn't say a good name is nice to have. He said it is more to be desired than great wealth. The man who had more wealth than almost anyone in history is telling you that your reputation is worth more than money.

Elsewhere, in the book of Ecclesiastes, he says it even more bluntly:

> *"A good name is better than a good ointment."*
> — Ecclesiastes 7:1 (NASB)

In Solomon's day, fragrant ointment was expensive. It was a luxury. A status symbol. He is saying your name — your character, your reputation — is worth more than the most valuable thing money can buy.

This is not a minor observation from a minor person. This is the concentrated wisdom of a man who tested everything life has to offer and reported back. When Solomon tells you something matters, you would be wise to listen.

Names That Outlasted the Women Who Carried Them

The Bible is filled with women whose names became something far greater than a label. Women who, by their choices, wrote a story with their lives that is still being told thousands of years later.

Consider a few:

Ruth — a Moabite widow with nothing. No husband, no children, no future. By every measure of her culture, she was finished. But when her mother-in-law Naomi decided to return to Israel, Ruth made a choice that would define her name forever:

> *"Do not urge me to leave you or turn back from following you; for where you go, I will go, and where you lodge, I will lodge. Your people shall be my people, and your God, my God."*
>
> — Ruth 1:16 (NASB)

That one act of loyalty — choosing faithfulness when it cost her everything — placed Ruth in the lineage of King David and, ultimately, of Jesus Christ Himself. A foreign widow with no prospects became an ancestor of the Messiah. Her name is still spoken with honor in every church, in every nation, wherever the Bible is read.

When Ruth's story came to its conclusion, the women of Bethlehem said to Naomi:

> *"May he also be to you a restorer of life and a sustainer of your old age; for your daughter-in-law, who loves you and is better to you than seven sons, has given birth to him."*
>
> — Ruth 4:15 (NASB)

Better than seven sons. In that culture, that was the highest compliment imaginable. Ruth's name had become something.

Rahab — a prostitute in the city of Jericho. By any human measure, her name should have been forgotten in shame. But when the Israelite spies came to her city, Rahab made a choice. She hid them. She lied to the king's men to protect them. And she confessed something remarkable:

> *"I know that the Lord has given you the land... for the Lord your God, He is God in heaven above and on earth beneath."*
> — Joshua 2:9, 11 (NASB)

That act of faith — risking her life for the God of Israel — transformed her name forever. Rahab was spared when Jericho fell. She married into the nation of Israel. And like Ruth, she appears in the genealogy of Jesus Christ. A prostitute, remembered for faith.

The book of Hebrews, listing the greatest examples of faith in all of Scripture, includes her:

> *"By faith Rahab the harlot did not perish along with those who were disobedient, after she had welcomed the spies in peace."*
> — Hebrews 11:31 (NASB)

Her past did not define her. Her faith did.

The woman with the alabaster jar — we don't even know her name. But Jesus made a promise about her that has been kept for two thousand years:

— Matthew 26:13 (NASB)

She poured out expensive perfume on Jesus' feet. The disciples criticized her for wasting it. But Jesus saw her heart. And He declared that her act of devotion would be remembered wherever the gospel is told.

We don't know her given name. But we know her story. We know what she did. And that — in God's economy — is her name.

Your Name Is Already Being Written

You may think you have time before any of this matters. You don't.

Every single day, in ways large and small, you are writing the story of your name. The people around you — your family, your friends, the people you work with, the young man you talk to, the teacher, the employer, the neighbor — are all forming an impression. And unlike what happens on a screen, that impression cannot be deleted.

Think about the people you already know. There are names you hear and immediately feel a sense of trust. And there are names you hear that make you instinctively a little more careful. You didn't sit down and analyze those people. You didn't study their resume. You accumulated experiences with them — or heard the experiences of people who know them — and your mind made a record.

Your name is being recorded in exactly the same way, right now, in the minds of everyone around you.

The question is not whether your name is being written.
It is what is being written.

What Actually Builds a Name

A good name is not built with big dramatic gestures. It is built in the small, ordinary, unspectacular moments that nobody photographs and nobody applauds.

It is built when you:

- Tell the truth when a lie would cost you nothing and the truth costs you something.

- Keep a secret that someone trusted you with, even when sharing it would make you feel important.

- Keep your word to someone who couldn't do anything to you if you broke it.

- Show up on time, every time, because you said you would.

- Treat people the same way whether they can do something for you or not.

- Refuse to join in when others are tearing someone down — even if staying silent costs you socially.

- Take responsibility for your mistakes instead of manufacturing reasons why it wasn't your fault.

None of these things will trend. None of them will get you followers. But every single one of them deposits something into the account of your name — and over time, that account either grows into something of real value, or it quietly empties out.

The Danger No One Is Warning You About

Here is something your grandmother's generation never had to worry about, but you do — and it needs to be said plainly:

> *Your digital life is part of your name now.*

What you post. What you share. What you think is funny at seventeen. What you say in anger or in hurt or just because everyone else is saying it. The photos, the comments, the accounts you follow, the things you laugh at publicly — all of it is being recorded. Permanently. And the world you are about to step into — employers, graduate schools, future relationships — has access to it.

The young woman who spent years building a reputation for kindness and integrity in her community can undo years of that work with a single careless post. The digital world has no mercy and no short memory.

Solomon had no internet. But he understood the principle perfectly:

> *"Like a city that is broken into and without walls is a man who has no control over his spirit."*
> — Proverbs 25:28 (NASB)

A person without self-control has no protection. Not in Solomon's day, and not in yours. The platform changes. The principle does not.

Guard your name online with the same seriousness you would guard it in person. Because to the world you are about to walk into, there is no difference.

Growing Into Your Name

Here is the most hopeful thing in this entire chapter:

Your name is not finished yet.

Rahab was a prostitute before she became a hero of faith. Ruth was a destitute widow before she became an ancestor of kings. The woman with the alabaster jar was known to be "a sinner" before Jesus declared her act would be remembered forever.

If your name carries some weight it shouldn't, it is not too late to change what you're writing. The same God who looked at a foreign widow and placed her in the line of His own Son is the same God who looks at you — exactly as you are — and sees what you could become.

But it starts with a decision. A daily decision. The decision to take your name seriously. To act like it matters. To understand that who you are when no one is watching is who you actually are — and that eventually, who you actually are becomes what everyone knows.

Proverbs 31, the passage that describes the woman of noble character, ends with this:

> *"Her children rise up and bless her; her husband also, and he praises her, saying: 'Many daughters have done nobly, but you excel them all.'"*
>
> — Proverbs 31:28–29 (NASB)

That is a name. That is a legacy. That is what a life well-lived produces — not likes, not followers, not applause from strangers, but the genuine honor of the people who know you best.

That kind of name is available to you. It is being written, right now, by the choices you make today.

For Further Study

Look these passages up yourself. Open a Bible — not a phone app, a Bible — and read the surrounding context:

- Proverbs 22:1

- Ecclesiastes 7:1

- Ruth 1:16–17 and Ruth 4:13–17

- Joshua 2:1–21 and Hebrews 11:31

- Matthew 26:6–13

- Proverbs 31:10–31

> *"A good name is to be more desired than great wealth; favor is better than silver and gold."*
>
> — Proverbs 22:1 (NASB)

CHAPTER 2

The Woman in the Mirror Isn't the Whole Story

Part One: Who You Are

You have been evaluated your entire life by what people can see.

Your appearance. Your weight. Your hair. Your clothes. Whether you're pretty enough, thin enough, stylish enough. Whether you smile the right way, wear the right things, and look the right way in photos. The world around you has been forming opinions about you since the day you were born — and almost every single one of those opinions has been based on what's visible on the outside.

The pressure is relentless. You know it is. Every filter, every angle, every carefully curated image — the message is always the same: your value is in what can be seen.

Here is what God says about that entire system of evaluation:

"God sees not as man sees, for man looks at the outward appearance, but the Lord looks at the heart."

— 1 Samuel 16:7 (NASB)

One sentence. And it dismantles the entire basis on which the world judges a woman.

God is not impressed by what you can perform. He is not moved by what you look like, how many people follow you, how well you present yourself, or how perfectly you can pose for a picture. He looks straight past all of it — past the image you've carefully constructed, past the version of yourself you put forward for other people — and He looks directly at your heart.

That should be both sobering and freeing. Sobering, because you cannot fool Him. Freeing, because the things that impress Him are available to every woman — regardless of appearance, popularity, or circumstances.

The Story Behind the Verse

That verse in 1 Samuel 16 comes from one of the most instructive moments in all of Scripture, and it's worth understanding the full picture.

God had told the prophet Samuel to go to the house of a man named Jesse, because one of Jesse's sons was going to be the next king of Israel. Samuel arrived and Jesse began presenting his sons. The first one to walk in was a young man named Eliab — and the text tells us that Samuel looked at him and thought, surely this is the one God has chosen. Eliab was tall. He was impressive. He looked exactly like what a king should look like.

God immediately corrected Samuel. "Do not look at his appearance or at the height of his stature, because I have rejected him." And then God said the words that have echoed through every generation since: "For God sees not as man sees, for man looks at the outward appearance, but the Lord looks at the heart."

Son after son walked past Samuel. Seven of Jesse's sons. Not one of them was chosen.

Finally Samuel asked — is this all of them? And Jesse said, well, there's the youngest. He's out in the field watching the sheep. Nobody had even thought to call him in. He wasn't in the room because nobody considered him a serious candidate.

That youngest son's name was David.

"Arise, anoint him; for this is he."

The man after God's own heart — the greatest king in Israel's history, the ancestor of Jesus Christ — was the one nobody thought to invite to the meeting. He was outside doing his job faithfully, with no audience, no applause, and no idea that everything was about to change.

That is not a coincidence. That is a pattern. God consistently chooses and uses people based on what is happening on the inside, not what is being performed on the outside.

What Scripture Says Directly to Women

The principle of 1 Samuel 16:7 applies to everyone. But the New Testament takes that truth and applies it directly to women in a passage that could not be more relevant to your generation:

> *"Your adornment must not be merely external — braiding the hair, and wearing gold jewelry, or putting on dresses; but let it be the hidden person of the heart, with the imperishable quality of a gentle and quiet spirit, which is precious in the sight of God."*
>
> — 1 Peter 3:3–4 (NASB)

Read that carefully. Peter is not saying it's wrong to braid your hair or wear jewelry or dress nicely. That's not the point. The point is that your adornment — the thing that makes you beautiful, the thing that gives you value — must not be merely external.

There is something deeper. Something hidden. Something imperishable.

The world's definition of beauty is perishable. It fades. It ages. It is chased desperately and lost inevitably. But the beauty Peter is describing — the hidden person of the heart — does not fade. It grows. It deepens. It becomes more valuable with time, not less.

And here is the part to read carefully:

> *It is precious in the sight of God.*

The God who created the universe, who hung the stars and painted the sunset — that God looks at a woman with a gentle and quiet spirit and calls her precious. Not her hair. Not her figure. Not her carefully edited photos. Her heart.

What Is the Heart?

When the Bible talks about the heart, it is not talking about the organ in your chest. In both Hebrew and Greek, the heart refers to the inner person — the seat of your will, your thoughts, your desires, your motives. It is the deepest, most private part of who you are. The part that no one else can see.

It is who you are when you are completely alone.

It is the thought behind the action. The motive behind the gesture. The reason you actually did the thing you did — not the reason you told other people.

And God sees it with perfect clarity.

"For the word of God is living and active, and sharper than any two-edged sword, and piercing as far as the division of soul and spirit, of both joints and marrow, and able to judge the thoughts and intentions of the heart."

— Hebrews 4:12 (NASB)

That verse is describing what God's Word does when it works on a person. It goes beneath the surface. It gets past the performance. It exposes what is actually there — the thoughts, yes, but also the intentions. Not just what you did, but why you did it.

This is why two women can do the exact same thing and it can mean something completely different to God. One woman serves others because she genuinely loves people and wants to honor God. Another woman serves others because she wants to be seen serving others. The action looks identical. The heart behind it is entirely different.

God knows which is which. Every time.

The Word Nobody Talks About Anymore

There is a word that used to be common in the vocabulary of women and has nearly disappeared from the modern world.

Integrity.

Integrity comes from the same root as the word integer — a whole number. A number that is not a fraction. Not divided. Complete.

A woman of integrity is not divided. She is the same person in public that she is in private. She is the same person when the stakes are high as when no one is paying attention. She does not have a performance version of herself and a real version of herself. What you see is what you get, every time, in every room, under every kind of pressure.

The book of Proverbs describes this kind of person:

> *"A righteous man who walks in his integrity — how blessed are his sons after him."*
> — Proverbs 20:7 (NASB)

Notice something remarkable in that verse. It doesn't just say the person is blessed. It says those who come after them are blessed. Your integrity — or the lack of it — does not stay contained to your own life. It flows forward. Into the people who come after you. Into the family you will one day have. Into the young women who will watch you and learn from you what a woman is supposed to look like.

You are already influencing someone younger than you. You may not be aware of it. But somewhere there is a girl who is watching the way you carry yourself — and forming her idea of womanhood based on what she sees.

What is she learning?

Who You Are When No One Is Watching

Here is a simple test for the condition of your heart. Ask yourself honestly:

How do I act when there is absolutely nothing to gain and no one to impress?

Do you treat people with kindness when they can do nothing for you — or only when it benefits you? Do you keep your word when breaking it would have no consequences — or only when someone is holding you accountable? Do you speak well of people when they're not in the room — or only when they can hear you?

These are not hypothetical questions. These are questions about the real you. The you that God sees at all times.

King David — the same young man God chose from a field, who nobody thought to invite into the room — wrote this:

> *"Search me, O God, and know my heart; try me and know my anxious thoughts; and see if there be any hurtful way in me, and lead me in the everlasting way."*
>
> — Psalm 139:23–24 (NASB)

That is a dangerous prayer. It is the prayer of someone who is willing to be examined. Who is not hiding behind a performance. Who understands that the condition of her heart matters more than the condition of her reputation.

Most people never pray that prayer because they're not sure they want the honest answer. But the women who can pray it — and mean it — are the women God can do something with.

The Slow Work of Building a Heart

Here is the truth that culture will never tell you: becoming a woman of genuine character is slow work. It does not happen all at once. It does not happen in a weekend retreat or after a powerful sermon or because you felt something deeply in the moment.

It happens the way a muscle is built — through repeated effort, day after day, in the ordinary moments where nobody is watching and nothing dramatic is happening.

- Every time you choose honesty over convenience, your heart gets a little stronger in that direction.

- Every time you choose to build someone up instead of tearing them down, something grows in you.

- Every time you refuse to gossip when everyone else is, something is being formed that will hold weight later.

- Every time you take responsibility for a failure instead of deflecting it, you are building something that will last.

And every time you do the opposite — every shortcut, every half-truth, every time you treat people differently based on what they can do for you — something erodes. Quietly. Without fanfare. But it erodes.

The writer of Proverbs said it this way:

"Watch over your heart with all diligence, for from it flow the springs of life."

— Proverbs 4:23 (NASB)

Watch over it with all diligence. Not occasionally. Not when it's convenient. With all diligence — which means it requires active, intentional, ongoing attention.

Your heart is not something that takes care of itself. It requires tending. And the primary tool for tending it is the Word of God — which is why this book will keep returning to Scripture, and why the challenge at the end of every chapter asks you to open a Bible and spend time in it.

You cannot build a healthy heart on a diet of social media, entertainment, and peer pressure. It simply cannot be done. The inputs shape the heart, and the heart shapes the woman.

Choose your inputs carefully.

For Further Study

Read the whole account — not just the famous verse. Let the full story land.

- 1 Samuel 16:1–13 — The choosing of David

- 1 Peter 3:1–6 — The full context of inner beauty

- Psalm 139:1–24 — David's meditation on what it means to be fully known by God

- Proverbs 4:20–27 — Guarding the heart

- Hebrews 4:12–13 — Nothing is hidden from God

"Let it be the hidden person of the heart, with the imperishable quality of a gentle and quiet spirit, which is precious in the sight of God."

— 1 Peter 3:4 (NASB)

CHAPTER 3

When Nobody's Watching Becomes When Everybody's Watching

Part One: Who You Are

There is a question that every young woman will eventually have to answer. Not once, but repeatedly, throughout her entire life. And the way she answers it — especially early on, especially when the cost is real — will determine more about the shape of her character than almost anything else.

The question is this:

> *Will you stand for what is right when standing costs you something?*

Not when it's easy. Not when everyone around you agrees. Not when the crowd is on your side and the wind is at your back. But when the most powerful people in the room are telling you to sit down — and sitting down would be so much simpler.

There was a young woman in the Bible who answered that question, and answered it well. Her story begins in the shadows of a foreign empire and ends with the salvation of an entire people. And it starts the same way most great stories of character start — not with a dramatic speech, not in a moment of high crisis, but in the quiet formation of faith before the test ever arrived.

Her name was Hadassah. You probably know her by her Persian name: Esther.

Taken

To understand what Esther faced, you have to understand what had happened to her people.

The Jews had been conquered and scattered. They lived as exiles in the Persian Empire — the largest empire the world had ever seen, stretching from India to Ethiopia. They were outsiders. Minorities. Vulnerable. And in that context, a young Jewish orphan named Hadassah was being raised by her older cousin Mordecai, who had adopted her as his own daughter.

Then the king of Persia, Ahasuerus, decided he wanted a new queen. A search was conducted throughout the empire. Young women were gathered from every province and brought to the palace. Esther was among them.

She was beautiful. She found favor with everyone who saw her. And when her turn came to appear before the king, she won his heart. The orphan girl became queen of the most powerful empire on earth.

But there was something the king didn't know. Esther was a Jew. Mordecai had instructed her not to reveal her identity, and she had obeyed. She kept her faith hidden, living in the palace, surrounded by luxury, holding a secret that would later cost her everything to reveal.

The Crisis

A man named Haman rose to power in the Persian court. He was arrogant, ambitious, and deeply insecure. When Mordecai — Esther's cousin, who sat at the king's gate — refused to bow down to him, Haman was furious. But destroying one man wasn't enough for him. When he learned that Mordecai was a Jew, he decided to destroy all of them.

Haman went to the king with a proposal:

> *"There is a certain people scattered and dispersed among the peoples in all the provinces of your kingdom; their laws are different from those of all other people and they do not observe the king's laws, so it is not in the king's interest to let them remain. If it is pleasing to the king, let it be decreed that they be destroyed."*
>
> — Esther 3:8–9 (NASB)

The king agreed. A decree was issued. On a specific day, every Jew in the empire — men, women, and children — was to be killed. Their property would be plundered. There would be no escape.

When Mordecai heard the news, he tore his clothes and put on sackcloth and ashes. He wept loudly in the middle of the city. The Jewish people throughout the empire went into mourning.

And Esther, in the palace, heard that something was wrong with her cousin. She sent clothes to him, but he refused them. She sent a messenger to find out what was happening.

Mordecai sent back the full report — the decree, the date, the plan. And he sent one more thing: a challenge.

For Such a Time as This

Mordecai's message to Esther contained some of the most piercing words in all of Scripture:

> *"Do not imagine that you in the king's palace can escape any more than all the Jews. For if you remain silent at this time, relief and deliverance will arise for the Jews from another place and you and your father's house will perish. And who knows whether you have not attained royalty for such a time as this?"*
>
> — Esther 4:13–14 (NASB)

Read that carefully. Mordecai was not giving her an easy out. He was not saying, "If you can't help, that's okay." He was saying: You will not escape. If you think your position protects you, you are wrong. You are a Jew too, and when they come for the Jews, they will come for you.

But then he added something else. Something that shifts everything:

> *"Who knows whether you have not attained royalty for such a time as this?"*

What if this is the reason? What if all of it — the beauty contest, the favor, the crown, the palace — was not about comfort or privilege at all? What if it was positioning? What if God had been moving pieces on a board for years, placing an orphan girl in the one place where she could stand between her people and annihilation?

That question should haunt every young woman reading this book. What if your circumstances — your talents, your position, your opportunities — are not random? What if you are where you are for such a time as this?

The Decision

Here is what you need to understand about Esther's situation: going to the king uninvited was a death sentence. Persian law was explicit. Anyone who approached the king in the inner court without being summoned would be put to death — unless the king extended his golden scepter. There were no exceptions. Not even for the queen.

Esther had not been summoned in thirty days. She had no guarantee the king would receive her. And even if he did, she would have to reveal her identity as a Jew — the very people who had just been marked for destruction.

She could stay silent. She could hope someone else would do something. She could protect herself.

Instead, she sent this message back to Mordecai:

> *"Go, assemble all the Jews who are found in Susa, and fast for me; do not eat or drink for three days, night or day. I and my maidens also will fast in the same way. And thus I will go in to the king, which is not according to the law; and if I perish, I perish."*
>
> — Esther 4:16 (NASB)

Read those last five words again:

"If I perish, I perish."

This is not bravado. This is not recklessness. This is the statement of a woman who has weighed the cost, counted it carefully, and decided that doing the right thing matters more than surviving.

She was not bargaining with God. She was not standing firm because she had a guarantee of safety. She was standing firm because it was right — regardless of the outcome. Her obedience was not conditional on God's deliverance. Her faithfulness was not a transaction.

> *That is a level of conviction that cannot be manufactured in a moment of crisis.*

It can only come from years of quieter, private faithfulness — exactly the kind Esther had been building in those hidden years when she kept her faith while living in a pagan palace, when she obeyed Mordecai's instruction, when she honored God in ways nobody recorded and nobody applauded.

The Result

Esther went to the king. He extended the scepter. She was received.

Over the course of two banquets, with extraordinary wisdom and courage, she revealed Haman's plot. She revealed her own identity. She pleaded for her people.

The king was furious — not at Esther, but at Haman. The man who had plotted genocide was hanged on the very gallows he had built for Mordecai. A new decree was issued allowing the Jews to defend themselves. And on the day that was supposed to be their destruction, they were victorious.

The Jewish people were saved. And they have celebrated that deliverance every year since, in a festival called Purim, named after the "pur" — the lot — that Haman had cast to choose the date of their destruction.

One woman's courage. One woman's willingness to stand when standing could cost her life. That is what stood between an entire people and extinction.

What This Means for You

You are probably not a queen. You are probably not facing a decree of genocide. But you are facing — and will continue to face — moments where standing for what is right will cost you something.

Maybe it will cost you a friendship. Maybe it will cost you popularity. Maybe it will cost you an opportunity, a relationship, a comfortable silence that would be so much easier to maintain.

Here is what Esther's story teaches:

- Private faithfulness prepares you for public tests. Esther's courage before the king was built in the hidden years of quiet obedience.

- Your position is not an accident. The opportunities, abilities, and circumstances you have may be preparation for something you cannot yet see.

- Silence is not neutral. When you have the ability to act and choose not to, that is a choice — and it has consequences.

- Courage is not the absence of fear. Esther was terrified. She fasted for three days. But she went anyway.

- Outcomes belong to God. Esther could not guarantee her survival. She could only guarantee her faithfulness. The results were God's business.

The young woman who practices standing for small things — who tells the truth when it's inconvenient, who refuses to participate in cruelty even when it's socially costly, who maintains her integrity when no one is watching — is building something. She is becoming the kind of woman who will be able to stand when the stakes are much, much higher.

> *Character is always built in private before it is tested in public.*

For Further Study

Read the whole book of Esther. It is short — only ten chapters — and it reads like a thriller. Let the full story land.

- Esther 1–2 — How Esther came to be queen

- Esther 3 — Haman's plot

- Esther 4 — Mordecai's challenge and Esther's decision

- Esther 5–7 — Esther's courage and Haman's downfall

- Esther 8–10 — The deliverance of the Jews

*"And who knows whether you
have not attained royalty for such a
time as this?"*

— Esther 4:14 (NASB)

CHAPTER 4

You Were Made On Purpose, For a Purpose

Part One: Who You Are

Somewhere along the way, the culture handed you a story about yourself.

It goes something like this: you are the product of random biological processes that nobody planned and nobody intended. You are here by accident. Your personality, your tendencies, your struggles — these are the result of genetics and environment and a long chain of events that had nothing to do with design. There is no blueprint. There is no designer. There is no purpose built into you that you didn't put there yourself.

And if that story is true, then your value is whatever the world decides it is. It can be measured in likes, in followers, in how you look compared to other women, in whether the right people approve of you. Your worth rises and falls with the opinions of people who don't even know you.

That is the story the modern world tells young women.

Here is what God says.

Before You Were Born

The prophet Jeremiah was young — probably a teenager — when God spoke to him. And the first thing God said to him was this:

> *"Before I formed you in the womb I knew you, and before you were born I consecrated you; I have appointed you a prophet to the nations."*
>
> — Jeremiah 1:5 (NASB)

Read that slowly. Three things happened before Jeremiah drew his first breath.

God formed him. Not passively, not accidentally — formed. The same word used in Genesis 2 when God formed Adam from the dust of the ground. Deliberate. Intentional. Hands-on.

God knew him. Not knew of him. Not knew about him. Knew him — personally, intimately, completely. Before a single cell had divided. Before his mother knew she was pregnant. God knew Jeremiah.

God consecrated him. Set him apart. Designated him for a specific purpose. Appointed him to a specific task.

Before Jeremiah had done a single thing — before he had succeeded or failed, impressed anyone or disappointed anyone, developed a single talent or revealed a single flaw — God had already designed him, known him, and set him apart.

> *That is not the story of an accident. That is the story of a plan.*

And what was true for Jeremiah is true for you.

The Psalm That Should Change How You See Yourself

King David — the same young man we met in Chapter 2, chosen from a field because God saw his heart — wrote one of the most extraordinary descriptions of human life ever put into words. It is Psalm 139, and if you have never read it in full, that is your assignment this week.

But for now, consider these verses:

> *"For You formed my inward parts; You wove me in my mother's womb. I will give thanks to You, for I am fearfully and wonderfully made; wonderful are Your works, and my soul knows it very well. My frame was not hidden from You, when I was made in secret, and skillfully wrought in the depths of the earth; Your eyes have seen my unformed substance; and in Your book were all written the days that were ordained for me, when as yet there was not one of them."*
>
> — Psalm 139:13–16 (NASB)

There is almost too much in those four verses to unpack fully, but stay with it.

"You formed my inward parts." The word translated "formed" here is the Hebrew word for a weaver — someone who works with threads, interlacing them with intention and skill. God did not assemble you carelessly. He wove you.

"I am fearfully and wonderfully made." The word "fearfully" here does not mean frightening. It means awe-inspiring. It means the work that went into making you is the kind of work that produces reverence in those who truly understand it. David is not being sentimental. He is making a theological statement: the complexity and intentionality of a human being, seen clearly, should produce awe.

"In Your book were all written the days that were ordained for me." Before you lived a single one of your days — God had already written them. Not in the sense that you have no choices or that nothing you do matters. But in the sense that you are not wandering through an empty universe with no map and no destination. You are a person with ordained days — days that God saw before you lived them.

> *That is not the biography of an accident. That is the biography of someone who was expected.*

What This Means When Life Doesn't Feel That Way

Here is where honesty is required, because some young women reading this are carrying things that make all of this hard to believe.

Maybe you look in the mirror and see someone who doesn't measure up. Maybe the comparison game has worn you down until you genuinely believe you are less valuable than the women you see on your screen.

Maybe you have been told, in ways spoken or unspoken, that you are not particularly valuable. That you are a burden, a problem, a disappointment. That you are too much or not enough — too loud or too quiet, too emotional or too cold, too ambitious or not ambitious enough.

Maybe you have made choices you are not proud of — and the idea that God designed you for a purpose feels like it belongs to someone else. Someone who has her act together. Someone who hasn't done what you have done.

Jeremiah himself struggled with this. When God told him he was consecrated as a prophet to the nations, Jeremiah's response was immediate and honest:

> *"Alas, Lord God! Behold, I do not know how to speak, because I am a youth."*
>
> — Jeremiah 1:6 (NASB)

He didn't feel qualified. He didn't feel ready. He looked at himself and saw limitations where God saw a calling.

God's answer was not a pep talk. It was a correction:

> *"Do not say, 'I am a youth,' because everywhere I send you, you shall go, and all that I command you, you shall speak. Do not be afraid of them, for I am with you to deliver you."*
>
> — Jeremiah 1:7–8 (NASB)

God did not say — you are actually more talented than you think. He said — the issue of your adequacy is not the point. I am sending you. I am with you. Go.

> *The purpose God has for a woman is not dependent on whether she feels worthy of it. It is dependent on whether she is willing to walk in it.*

The Designer Left a Manual

Here is a simple truth that gets lost in a world full of noise:

When something is designed, the designer understands it better than anyone else. Better than the people who use it. Better than the critics who evaluate it. Better than the person who owns it.

If you want to understand what something is for — what it was built to do, how it works best, what will damage it, what will make it thrive — you go to the designer.

God designed you. And He did not leave you without a Word.

The Bible is not a collection of ancient rules invented by religious people trying to control other people. It is the instruction manual written by the One who made you — who knows exactly how you are wired, exactly what you need, exactly what will build you up and exactly what will tear you apart.

When the Bible says don't do a certain thing, it is not arbitrary restriction. It is the Designer telling you — that will damage what I built. When it says pursue a certain thing, it is the Designer telling you — that is what you were made for. That is where you will find what you are actually looking for.

> *"Your word is a lamp to my feet and a light to my path."*
> — Psalm 119:105 (NASB)

A lamp doesn't illuminate everything at once. It illuminates the next step. And then the step after that. You don't have to see the end of the road to walk faithfully on it. You just have to stay close enough to the light to see where to put your foot next.

That is what this book is trying to help you do — stay close enough to God's Word that the next step is always lit.

Purpose Is Not a Feeling

One more thing before this chapter closes, and it is important.

A lot of young women are waiting to feel their purpose before they pursue it. They are waiting for clarity, for passion, for the unmistakable sense that this is what I am meant to do. And in the meantime, they drift. They fill the waiting with scrolling and distractions and the slow erosion of days that could have been building something.

Or they wait for someone else to give their life meaning — the right relationship, the right opportunity, the right person to notice them. As if purpose is something that arrives from outside rather than something that is walked out from within.

Purpose, in the biblical sense, is not primarily a feeling. It is a direction.

The direction is this: know God, reflect His character, serve the people around you, and do your work with everything you have. That is true for every woman, in every season, regardless of whether she has figured out her career path or her life plan or her unique calling.

Ecclesiastes 9:10 says it plainly:

"Whatever your hand finds to do, do it with all your might."
— Ecclesiastes 9:10 (NASB)

Not whatever your hand finds to do that excites you. Not whatever your hand finds to do that feels meaningful at the moment. Whatever your hand finds to do — do it fully. Completely. As unto God.

The young woman who is faithful in the small, unglamorous, unexciting work in front of her right now is the young woman who will be trusted with more. That is not just wisdom. That is the direct teaching of Jesus in the parable of the talents — Matthew 25:14–30 — which is worth reading this week.

> *You were made on purpose.*

> *You were made for a purpose.*

The first step toward that purpose is not finding it. It is being faithful right where you are.

For Further Study

Read the full chapters. Let the weight of what God says about you settle in.

- Psalm 139:1–24 — David's meditation on being fully known and wonderfully made
- Jeremiah 1:1–19 — Jeremiah's call, hesitation, and God's response
- Ephesians 2:10 — "We are His workmanship, created in Christ Jesus for good works"
- Matthew 25:14–30 — The parable of the talents

"I will give thanks to You, for I am fearfully and wonderfully made; wonderful are Your works, and my soul knows it very well."

— Psalm 139:14 (NASB)

CHAPTER 5

The Relationship You Actually Need Most

Part Two: Who God Is

The world has been selling you a story about relationships since before you could spell your own name.

It goes something like this: somewhere out there is a person — the right person — and when you find them, everything will make sense. You will feel complete. The ache you carry, the restlessness, the sense that something is missing — all of it will resolve when you meet the one who was made for you. Your job is to find that person, or to make yourself findable, and then your life will really begin.

Movies teach you this. Songs teach you this. Even well-meaning people teach you this when they ask whether you have a boyfriend before they ask about anything else, as though nothing you do quite counts until you have found someone to do it with.

There is a truth buried in there — you were made for relationship. But the lie wrapped around that truth has sent countless young women chasing the wrong thing in the wrong places.

> *There is a relationship you need more than any other.*
> *And it is not with a man.*

The One Thing Necessary

Jesus was traveling with His disciples when they came to a village called Bethany, just outside Jerusalem. A woman named Martha lived there with her sister Mary, and Martha opened her home to Jesus.

What happens next is one of the most misunderstood scenes in the Gospels.

> *"Now as they were traveling along, He entered a village; and a woman named Martha welcomed Him into her home. She had a sister called Mary, who was seated at the Lord's feet, listening to His word. But Martha was distracted with all her preparations; and she came up to Him and said, 'Lord, do You not care that my sister has left me to do all the serving alone? Then tell her to help me.'"*
>
> — Luke 10:38–40 (NASB)

Picture this scene. Martha has welcomed Jesus into her home — which is an act of hospitality, an act of service, a good thing. In that culture, hosting a rabbi and his disciples meant providing food, drink, places to sit, all the practical needs of a group of travelers. Martha is doing exactly what a faithful, hardworking woman should do.

Meanwhile, Mary is sitting at Jesus' feet.

That phrase — "seated at the Lord's feet" — is a technical term. It describes the posture of a student learning from a rabbi. Mary is not being lazy. She is not neglecting her duties because she cannot be bothered. She is doing something radical: she is taking the position of a disciple.

And Martha is furious.

"Lord, do You not care?" She does not ask Mary to come help. She asks Jesus to make Mary help. She wants the authority figure to put things back in their proper order — women in the kitchen, practical needs attended to, everything running the way it should.

Listen to how Jesus responds:

> *"Martha, Martha, you are worried and bothered about so many things; but only one thing is necessary, for Mary has chosen the good part, which shall not be taken away from her."*
> — Luke 10:41–42 (NASB)

Jesus does not say Martha's work is bad. He does not criticize hospitality. He says Martha is "worried and bothered about so many things" — distracted, pulled in multiple directions, serving out of anxiety rather than rest.

And then He says the words that should reshape how every young woman thinks about priorities:

> *"Only one thing is necessary."*

Not many things. Not a balance of things. One thing.

Mary chose it. And Jesus says it will not be taken from her.

What Mary Understood

Here is what Mary understood that Martha had not yet grasped: Jesus would not always be there.

The preparations could wait. The meal could be delayed. The practical concerns of hospitality would be there tomorrow. But Jesus, sitting in that room, speaking words of life — this moment was finite. This opportunity would pass.

Mary saw what was actually in front of her and responded to it. Martha saw what was in front of her and let anxiety about other things distract her from it.

This is not a story about whether women should work or rest. This is not a story about personality types. This is a story about what matters most — and whether you will choose it when it is right in front of you.

The relationship with Jesus was what mattered most. Mary chose it. And Jesus defended her choice.

The Woman at the Well

There is another woman in the Gospels whose encounter with Jesus changed everything — and her story is even more striking.

She was a Samaritan, which already put her outside respectable Jewish society. Jews and Samaritans did not associate with one another — the hostility between the two groups went back centuries. She was a woman, which meant that a rabbi would not normally speak to her in public. And she came to draw water at noon, the hottest part of the day, when the other women would not be there.

That detail tells you something. Women drew water in the morning or evening, when it was cooler, and they went together. This woman came alone, at the worst possible time. She was avoiding people.

John's Gospel tells us why: she had been married five times, and the man she was living with now was not her husband.

We do not know the full story — whether she had been abandoned, widowed, or made choices she regretted. What we know is that she carried a weight of shame heavy enough to reshape her daily routine. She arranged her life to avoid the stares and whispers of other women.

And then she met Jesus at the well.

> *"There came a woman of Samaria to draw water. Jesus said to her, 'Give Me a drink.'… The Samaritan woman said to Him, 'How is it that You, being a Jew, ask me for a drink since I am a Samaritan woman?'"*
>
> — John 4:7, 9 (NASB)

She expected rejection, or at best, silence. What she got was a conversation that would change her life.

Living Water

Jesus said something to this woman that He said to very few people so directly:

> *"If you knew the gift of God, and who it is who says to you, 'Give Me a drink,' you would have asked Him, and He would have given you living water."*
>
> — John 4:10 (NASB)

She did not understand at first. She looked at the well, looked at Jesus, and pointed out the obvious: He had no waterpot, and the well was deep. How could He give her water?

But Jesus was not talking about the well.

"Everyone who drinks of this water will thirst again; but whoever drinks of the water that I will give him shall never thirst; but the water that I will give him will become in him a well of water springing up to eternal life."

— John 4:13–14 (NASB)

She had come to the well because she was thirsty. She came back every day because she was thirsty again. That is how ordinary water works — it satisfies for a moment, and then the need returns.

The same was true of everything she had pursued in life. Five husbands. Each one, perhaps, had seemed like the answer — the man who would finally satisfy, who would finally give her life meaning, who would finally fill the emptiness. And each time, the thirst returned.

Jesus was offering something different: water that would become a spring inside her. Not a temporary fix, but a permanent source. Not something she had to keep coming back for, but something that would flow from within.

> *That is what a relationship with Jesus offers that no human relationship can.*

She Left Her Waterpot

The conversation continued. Jesus revealed that He knew her past — all of it. She recognized Him first as a prophet, then began to wonder if He was something more. And then Jesus told her plainly what He rarely said so directly:

"The woman said to Him, 'I know that Messiah is coming (He who is called Christ); when that One comes, He will declare all things to us.' Jesus said to her, 'I who speak to you am He.'"

— John 4:25–26 (NASB)

This was the moment. The woman who had been avoiding people, hiding from shame, arranging her life around the stares of others — she had just been told, face to face, that the Messiah was standing in front of her.

And then something remarkable happened:

"So the woman left her waterpot, and went into the city and said to the people, 'Come, see a man who told me all the things that I have done; this is not the Christ, is it?'"

— John 4:28–29 (NASB)

Do not miss this.

She left her waterpot.

She came to the well for water. That was the whole reason she had walked to this place, in the heat of the day, alone. And when she met Jesus, she forgot the waterpot.

The thing she came for suddenly did not matter anymore.

And the woman who had arranged her entire day to avoid people ran into the city to tell everyone she could find.

That is what happens when you meet the Living Water. The old thirsts lose their power.

What This Means for You

Young women today are thirsty.

You are thirsty for attention, for validation, for someone to see you and choose you. You are thirsty for a relationship that will make you feel complete. You are thirsty for meaning, for purpose, for some sense that your life matters.

And the world keeps handing you cups of ordinary water — relationships that satisfy for a season and then leave you empty again. Attention that feels good until it doesn't. Validation that evaporates the moment someone newer or shinier comes along.

You keep coming back to the well because the thirst returns.

Jesus is offering something different.

He is offering a relationship that does not depend on your performance, your appearance, or your ability to keep someone interested. He is offering a love that knows your past — all of it — and does not walk away. He is offering living water: a source of life that springs up from within, that does not run dry, that transforms you from the inside out.

Mary sat at His feet because she understood that being with Jesus was the one thing necessary.

The Samaritan woman left her waterpot because she had found something better.

> *The relationship you actually need most is not with a man. It is with the Son of God.*

What It Means to Sit at His Feet

If Mary were alive today, what would sitting at Jesus' feet look like?

She could not literally sit in His physical presence — but you can do what she was doing. She was listening to His word. She was positioning herself to learn from Him. She was choosing His presence over distraction.

For you, that means opening the Scriptures and actually reading them. Not skimming. Not waiting for someone to summarize them for you. Reading the words of Jesus for yourself, slowly enough to hear them.

It means prayer — not as a ritual, but as conversation. Talking to Him. Listening for Him. Making time for Him the way you would make time for anyone whose relationship you valued.

It means choosing Him when there are a hundred other things pulling at your attention. The phone, the feed, the endless scroll of distraction — Martha's preparations looked different in the first century, but the principle is the same. Only one thing is necessary. Will you choose it?

It means believing that knowing Christ is better than anything you might miss out on by pursuing Him. Mary chose the good part. She was not punished for it. She was defended.

The Relationship That Changes Everything Else

Here is what happens when you get this relationship right: every other relationship falls into its proper place.

When you are not thirsty anymore, you stop demanding that other people fill a void they were never designed to fill. You can love a man without needing him to complete you. You can enjoy friendships without requiring them to be your ultimate source of validation. You can pursue your work without it becoming your identity.

The Samaritan woman stopped hiding. She stopped arranging her life around shame. She ran toward people instead of away from them.

That is what happens when you encounter Jesus. The fear loosens its grip. The shame loses its power. You are no longer defined by what you have done or what has been done to you. You are defined by whose you are.

And when some young man comes along who seems like he might be worth your attention, you will have the clarity to see him for what he is: a fellow human being, not a savior. A possible companion, not a source of salvation. Someone to walk with, not someone to worship.

> *The young woman who knows Jesus will not settle for less than she deserves — because she knows what she is worth.*

> *One thing is necessary.*

> *Living water is available.*

Choose the good part. Leave the waterpot behind.

For Further Study

Read the full accounts. Watch how Jesus speaks to women — with respect, with truth, with invitation.

- Luke 10:38–42 — Mary and Martha; the one thing necessary

- John 4:1–42 — The woman at the well; living water

- John 15:1–11 — Abiding in Christ; remaining in the vine

- Philippians 3:7–11 — Paul counts all things loss compared to knowing Christ

> *"Only one thing is necessary, for*
> *Mary has chosen the good part, which*
> *shall not be taken away from her."*
>
> — Luke 10:42 (NASB)

The Bible Isn't What You Think It Is

Part Two: Who God Is

If you have grown up around church, you have probably heard a lot of things about the Bible.

You have heard it is important. You have heard you should read it. You have heard it called "the Good Book" and "God's Word" and "the Scriptures." You have probably been handed one at some point — maybe with your name engraved on the cover — and told that it contains everything you need.

And then, if you are honest, you opened it and found something confusing. Genealogies. Laws about livestock. Prophecies full of imagery you did not understand. A man swallowed by a fish. Another man told to marry a prostitute. Stories that seemed strange, commands that seemed harsh, and long stretches that seemed boring.

So you closed it. Or you kept it on your nightstand and felt guilty for not reading it. Or you read little bits here and there — a Psalm when you felt sad, a Proverb when you needed wisdom — but never really understood how it all fit together.

If that describes you, you are not alone. And you are not stupid. The Bible is not a simple book. It was written over fifteen hundred years by dozens of authors in three languages across multiple continents. It contains history, poetry, law, prophecy, letters, and apocalyptic visions. It does not read like a novel because it is not a novel.

But here is what you may not have been told:

> *The Bible is not what you think it is. It is more.*

What the Bible Says About Itself

Before we talk about how to read the Bible, we need to understand what it claims to be. And the clearest statement comes from Paul, writing to a young man named Timothy:

> *"All Scripture is inspired by God and profitable for teaching, for reproof, for correction, for training in righteousness; so that the man of God may be adequate, equipped for every good work."*
>
> — 2 Timothy 3:16–17 (NASB)

That is one of the most important sentences ever written about the Bible. Every word matters.

"All Scripture." Not some of it. Not the parts that feel inspiring or make sense to modern readers. All of it — from Genesis to Revelation, from the genealogies to the prophecies, from the laws you do not understand to the letters you do.

"Inspired by God." The Greek word here is theopneustos — literally, "God-breathed." This does not mean the Bible contains good ideas about God. It means the Bible comes from God. The words on the page are His words, breathed out through human authors who wrote exactly what He intended.

"Profitable." Useful. Beneficial. Not just for scholars or preachers, but for you — for teaching you what is true, reproving you when you are wrong, correcting your course, and training you in how to live.

"Equipped for every good work." The Bible is sufficient. It gives you everything you need to live the life God has called you to live. Not everything you are curious about, but everything you need.

This is not a book that contains some helpful suggestions alongside human opinions. This is God speaking.

Living and Active

There is another passage that describes what the Bible actually is:

> *"For the word of God is living and active and sharper than any two-edged sword, and piercing as far as the division of soul and spirit, of both joints and marrow, and able to judge the thoughts and intentions of the heart."*
>
> — Hebrews 4:12 (NASB)

Living. Not dead. Not a relic from an ancient world that no longer applies. The Bible is alive in a way no other book is alive. When you read it, something is happening that does not happen when you read anything else.

Active. Not passive. The Bible does not sit there waiting for you to do something with it. It does something to you. It works on you. It exposes things you did not know were there.

Sharper than any two-edged sword. This is not comfortable language. A sword cuts. A sword divides. The Bible is not a pillow to make you feel better about yourself. It is a surgical instrument that separates truth from lies, right from wrong, what you pretend to be from what you actually are.

Piercing as far as the division of soul and spirit. It reaches places nothing else can reach. Your innermost thoughts. Your hidden motives. The things you do not even admit to yourself.

Able to judge the thoughts and intentions of the heart. When you read the Bible honestly, it reads you back.

> *That is why some people avoid it. It is too close. It sees too much.*

What the Bible Is Not

To understand what the Bible is, it helps to clear away what it is not.

The Bible is not a rule book. Yes, it contains commands. Yes, God tells us what to do and what not to do. But if you think the Bible is primarily a list of rules, you have missed the point entirely. The Bible is the story of God rescuing a people for Himself — and the commands make sense only inside that story. They are not arbitrary restrictions. They are the Designer telling you how life works.

The Bible is not a self-help book. It will not give you five steps to a better you. It is not interested in helping you achieve your goals or maximize your potential. It is interested in something far more important: showing you who God is, who you are, and what has gone wrong between you.

The Bible is not a collection of inspirational quotes. You cannot treat it like a fortune cookie, cracking it open to find a feel-good message for your day. The verses people put on coffee mugs and wall art are real — but they mean something specific in their context, and ripping them out of that context often distorts what God actually said.

The Bible is not outdated. "That was written two thousand years ago" is not an argument against its relevance. Human nature has not changed. The heart is still deceitful. People still struggle with the same sins, the same fears, the same questions. And God, who does not change, still speaks through the words He breathed out.

What the Bible Actually Is

So what is the Bible, if it is not a rule book or a self-help guide or a collection of inspirational quotes?

The Bible is a revelation. It reveals things you could not know otherwise — who God is, what He has done, what He requires, what He promises. Without it, you would be guessing about the most important questions in the universe. With it, you have answers from the only One who actually knows.

The Bible is a story. It has a beginning (creation), a conflict (the fall), a resolution (redemption through Christ), and an ending (restoration). Every book fits somewhere in that story. Every passage makes more sense when you understand where it sits in the larger narrative.

The Bible is an invitation. It invites you to know God — not just to know about Him, but to know Him personally. The same God who spoke the universe into existence speaks to you through these pages. That is extraordinary. That is worth your attention.

And the Bible is enough. You do not need additional revelations, private messages, or new books to supplement what God has already said. What you need is to understand what He has already given you.

> *"The grass withers, the flower fades, but the word of our God stands forever."*
>
> — Isaiah 40:8 (NASB)

Why This Matters for You

Here is why all of this matters for a young woman trying to figure out her life:

You are bombarded every day with messages telling you who to be, what to want, and how to live. Social media tells you one thing. Movies tell you another. Your friends have opinions. Your family has expectations. The culture shifts constantly, and what was celebrated yesterday is condemned today.

In the middle of all that noise, there is one voice that does not change. One source that tells you the truth about yourself, about the world, and about God — not because it is one opinion among many, but because it comes from the One who made you and knows how you work.

If you want wisdom — real wisdom, the kind that will keep you from the traps other young women fall into — it is here.

If you want to know what is actually true about love, relationships, beauty, purpose, and meaning — it is here.

If you want to hear from God Himself, not filtered through someone else's opinions or watered down to make you comfortable — it is here.

How to Actually Read It

If you have tried to read the Bible and given up, here is some practical advice.

Start with the Gospels. Matthew, Mark, Luke, and John tell the story of Jesus — His life, His teaching, His death, and His resurrection. If you do not know Jesus, you will not understand anything else. Start there.

Read whole books, not just verses. The Bible was not written as a collection of disconnected verses. Each book has an author, an audience, and a purpose. When you read a verse in isolation, you can easily miss what it actually means. Read the chapter. Read the book. Let the context do its work.

Ask the right questions. When you read any passage, ask: Who is speaking? To whom? Under what circumstances? What comes before and after? These questions will save you from a hundred misunderstandings.

Let Scripture interpret Scripture. If a passage confuses you, look for other passages that address the same topic. The Bible does not contradict itself, and clear passages help explain difficult ones.

Read it expecting to be changed. Do not come to the Bible looking for confirmation of what you already believe. Come looking for truth, even if it challenges you. If the Bible never corrects you, you are probably not reading it honestly.

Read it regularly. You do not get to know someone through occasional contact. You get to know them by spending time with them consistently. The same is true with God's Word. Daily is better than weekly. Weekly is better than never. Build the habit.

The Book That Reads You

Here is the uncomfortable truth: when you open the Bible, you are not just reading it. It is reading you.

It will expose your selfishness when you wanted to believe you were generous. It will reveal your pride when you thought you were humble. It will show you that the things you thought were fine are actually sin, and the things you thought were impossible are actually commanded.

That is why people close it. That is why they make excuses not to read it. It is easier to stay in the dark than to let the light show you what is really there.

But the exposure is not cruelty. It is mercy. A doctor who diagnoses your disease is not your enemy. He is the one who can help you get well. The Bible shows you what is wrong so that you can be healed.

> *The young woman who reads God's Word daily will not be easily deceived.*

She will recognize lies because she knows the truth. She will see through the culture's empty promises because she has tasted something real. She will have a foundation that does not shift when everything around her is shifting.

That young woman could be you.

> *The Bible is not what you think it is.*

Open it. Read it. Let it read you back.

For Further Study

Spend time in these passages. Let the Bible make its own case for what it is.

- 2 Timothy 3:14–17 — The full context of Paul's words to Timothy about Scripture

- Hebrews 4:12–13 — The living, active, piercing Word

- Psalm 119:1–176 — The longest chapter in the Bible, entirely about God's Word

- 2 Peter 1:19–21 — How Scripture came to be

> *"All Scripture is inspired by God and profitable for teaching, for reproof, for correction, for training in righteousness; so that the man of God may be adequate, equipped for every good work."*
>
> — 2 Timothy 3:16–17 (NASB)

CHAPTER 7

Putting Down the Phone Long Enough to Hear Something True

Part Two: Who God Is

You already know what I am going to say.

You know it because you have felt it. That restless feeling when you have not checked your phone in ten minutes. That impulse to reach for it the moment you are bored, or uncomfortable, or alone with your thoughts. That sense that you are missing something if you are not scrolling, not watching, not connected.

You know the way time disappears. You pick up your phone to check one thing, and an hour later you are still there, having accomplished nothing except feeding an appetite that is never satisfied.

You know the way it makes you feel afterward. The comparison. The envy. The vague sense that everyone else is living a better life than you, even though you know — you know — that what you are seeing is not real.

I am not here to lecture you about screen time. You have heard those lectures. They have not changed anything, because lectures rarely do.

I am here to tell you what you are losing. And what you could have instead.

The God Who Speaks in Stillness

There is a verse in the Psalms that is often quoted but rarely obeyed:

> *"Cease striving and know that I am God."*
> — Psalm 46:10 (NASB)

Other translations say "Be still." The Hebrew word carries the idea of letting go, relaxing your grip, stopping your frantic activity. It is a command — not a suggestion.

Be still. Stop. Let go.

And then — know that I am God.

There is a connection between these two things. The stillness is not the point by itself. The stillness creates space for something else: knowing God. Hearing Him. Recognizing who He actually is.

But here is the problem: stillness has become almost impossible.

Every quiet moment is filled with noise. Every pause is interrupted by a notification. Every space that could be used for reflection is crammed with content — images, videos, posts, stories, messages, an endless stream of input that leaves no room for anything else.

> *You cannot hear a still, small voice when you are drowning in noise.*

Elijah and the Sound of Silence

There is a story in the Old Testament about a prophet named Elijah. He had just experienced one of the greatest victories in Israel's history — a dramatic confrontation with the prophets of Baal on Mount Carmel, where God sent fire from heaven and proved that He alone was the true God.

And then, almost immediately, Elijah was running for his life. Queen Jezebel had threatened to kill him, and he fled into the wilderness, afraid and exhausted and ready to give up.

God met him there. But not the way you might expect.

> *"So He said, 'Go forth and stand on the mountain before the Lord.' And behold, the Lord was passing by! And a great and strong wind was rending the mountains and breaking in pieces the rocks before the Lord; but the Lord was not in the wind. And after the wind an earthquake, but the Lord was not in the earthquake. After the earthquake a fire, but the Lord was not in the fire; and after the fire a sound of a gentle blowing."*
>
> — 1 Kings 19:11–12 (NASB)

Wind. Earthquake. Fire. All the dramatic, attention-grabbing phenomena you might expect from the God who had just called down fire on Mount Carmel.

But God was not in any of them.

God was in the sound of a gentle blowing. Some translations say "a still small voice." Others say "sheer silence." The Hebrew phrase is difficult to translate precisely, but the meaning is clear: God spoke in the quiet. He revealed Himself not in the spectacular but in the subtle.

Elijah had to be still enough to hear it.

> *What would you miss if you were scrolling through the wind, the earthquake, and the fire?*

What the Phone Is Actually Doing

Let me be direct with you about what is happening when you spend hours on your phone.

Your attention is being sold. The apps you use are not free. You pay for them with your time, your focus, and your mental energy. Companies have spent billions of dollars figuring out how to keep you engaged — not because they care about you, but because your attention is worth money to advertisers. Every feature is designed to make it harder for you to put the phone down.

Your emotions are being manipulated. The content that gets the most engagement is the content that triggers strong emotions — outrage, envy, fear, longing. You are not seeing a neutral picture of reality. You are seeing what is most likely to provoke a reaction. And those reactions are shaping you in ways you do not fully realize.

Your capacity for stillness is being destroyed. The more you fill every quiet moment with stimulation, the less able you become to tolerate silence. It is like a muscle that atrophies from disuse. You may have noticed that you feel uncomfortable when you do not have your phone — anxious, restless, like something is missing. That is not an accident. That is what happens when your brain has been trained to expect constant input.

Your sense of reality is being distorted. The lives you see on your screen are curated, filtered, and edited. The people you compare yourself to are showing you their highlight reel while you live in your behind-the-scenes. This is obvious when you think about it, but it does not feel obvious when you are scrolling. The comparison happens automatically, below the level of conscious thought.

And here is the hardest truth: the more time you spend in that world, the less time you have for the things that actually matter.

What You Are Missing

Every hour you spend scrolling is an hour you did not spend reading. Thinking. Praying. Being present with the people in front of you. Developing a skill. Creating something. Sitting with your own thoughts long enough to actually know yourself.

These are not small losses.

The young woman who never reads deeply will never think deeply. Her mind will be shaped by whatever content the algorithm serves her, which is designed to be consumed quickly and forgotten immediately.

The young woman who never prays — who never sits in silence long enough to talk to God and listen for His voice — will never develop the relationship that Chapter 5 talked about. She may know about Jesus, but she will not know Him.

The young woman who is never present — whose body is in the room but whose attention is somewhere else — will find that her relationships are shallow. People can tell when you are not really there. They feel it, even if they cannot name it.

The young woman who fills every quiet moment with noise will never hear the still small voice. She will miss the very thing she is searching for.

> *You cannot scroll your way to wisdom. You cannot swipe your way to peace.*

The Discipline of Silence

Here is what I am asking you to consider: silence is a discipline. It does not come naturally anymore — not in a world engineered to prevent it. You will have to fight for it.

Start small. Set aside ten minutes a day when you put the phone in another room and sit in silence. No music. No background noise. Just you and your thoughts. At first, this will feel uncomfortable. Your mind will race. You will feel the pull to check something, anything. That discomfort is exactly why you need to do it.

Use the silence to pray. Talk to God out loud or in your mind. Tell Him what you are thinking. Tell Him what you are afraid of. Tell Him what you want. And then be quiet long enough to listen — not for an audible voice, but for the impressions, the clarity, the peace that comes when you make space for Him.

Use the silence to read. Open your Bible and read slowly. A chapter. A paragraph. A single verse, if that is all you can manage. But read it without your phone nearby. Let the words sink in without the competition of notifications.

Increase the time as you are able. What feels impossible at first becomes easier with practice. The muscle of stillness can be rebuilt. But it takes intention. It takes saying no to something easy in order to say yes to something better.

What Stillness Gives You

Here is what you gain when you learn to be still:

Clarity. When the noise stops, you can finally hear yourself think. You can sort through what you actually believe, what you actually want, what actually matters. The confusion that comes from constant input begins to lift.

Peace. Not the absence of problems, but the presence of something deeper. The kind of peace that does not depend on circumstances, because it comes from knowing who God is and trusting that He is in control.

> *"Be anxious for nothing, but in everything by prayer and supplication with thanksgiving let your requests be made known to God. And the peace of God, which surpasses all comprehension, will guard your hearts and your minds in Christ Jesus."*
> — Philippians 4:6–7 (NASB)

Depth. Shallow input produces shallow people. But when you make space for deep reading, deep thinking, and deep conversation with God, you become someone with substance. You have something to offer that the scroll-addicted world does not.

Presence. When you are not mentally somewhere else, you can actually be where you are. The people around you will notice. Your conversations will be richer. Your relationships will be stronger. You will stop missing your own life because you were too busy watching other people's.

A Challenge

I am not asking you to throw your phone away. I am not pretending that technology is evil or that screens are sinful. There are good uses for these tools.

But tools are meant to serve you, not master you. And if you are honest, you know which one is happening in your life.

So here is a challenge: one week. For one week, put boundaries around your phone use. Set specific times when you will check it and specific times when it stays in another room. Replace at least some of your scrolling time with reading, praying, or simply sitting in silence.

Notice what happens. Notice how hard it is at first, and notice what becomes possible as you make space for stillness.

You may discover that the thing you thought you could not live without was actually the thing keeping you from what you needed most.

Be still.

Know that He is God.

You cannot hear the still small voice if you never stop to listen.

For Further Study

Sit with these passages. Read them slowly, without your phone nearby.

- Psalm 46:1–11 — The full context of "Be still and know"

- 1 Kings 19:1–18 — Elijah, the still small voice, and God's presence in the quiet

- Philippians 4:4–9 — Rejoicing, prayer, and the peace that guards your heart

• Psalm 1:1–6 — The blessed one who meditates on God's Word day and night

> *"Cease striving and know that I am God; I will be exalted among the nations, I will be exalted in the earth."*
>
> — Psalm 46:10 (NASB)

CHAPTER 8

He Is Somebody's Son

Part Three: How You Walk With People

Somewhere out there is a mother who raised the young man you will one day marry.

She held him when he was born. She watched him take his first steps. She sat up with him when he was sick, helped him with his homework, worried about him when he walked out the door. She prayed for him. She dreamed about who he would become.

And somewhere in those prayers, whether she said it out loud or not, she was also praying for you. For the young woman who would one day love her son. For the girl who would treat him with respect, who would be worthy of his heart, who would build him up instead of tearing him down.

She does not know your name yet. But she is hoping you exist.

I am telling you this because it is easy to forget that the young men you interact with are real people with real futures. They are not characters in your story, existing only to make you feel wanted or admired. They are not disposable — to be used for attention, entertainment, or validation and then discarded when someone more interesting comes along.

Every young man you meet is somebody's son. And he may be somebody's husband.

What Scripture Actually Says

The apostle Paul gave instructions to a young preacher named Timothy about how to treat people in the church. The words apply far beyond that original context:

> *"Do not sharply rebuke an older man, but rather appeal to him as a father, to the younger men as brothers, the older women as mothers, and the younger women as sisters, in all purity."*
> — 1 Timothy 5:1–2 (NASB)

Did you catch that phrase? Younger men as brothers. In all purity.

This is not just about what you do physically. Purity is a posture of the heart. It is about how you see someone, how you think about them, how you treat them. It means refusing to use another person for your own gratification — whether that gratification is physical, emotional, or social.

Treat him as a brother. That is the standard.

You would not manipulate your brother to get attention. You would not dress to provoke your brother. You would not play games with your brother's emotions to see if you could make him want you. You would not use your brother and then walk away when you got what you wanted.

A brother is someone you respect. Someone whose good you genuinely want. Someone you would never intentionally harm.

> *That is how you are called to treat every young man — whether you are interested in him or not.*

The Games That Harm

Let me name some things that need to be named.

Leading someone on. This happens when you enjoy the attention someone gives you but have no intention of returning their interest. You keep them close enough to keep giving you what you want — the compliments, the pursuit, the feeling of being desired — but you never tell them the truth. You let them hope because their hope benefits you.

That is not kindness. That is using a person.

Collecting admirers. Some young women measure their worth by how many young men they can attract. They flirt without intention, keep multiple possibilities dangling, and enjoy the power of being wanted. But attention is not the same as love, and the ability to attract someone is not the same as the character to deserve them.

Provoking desire you do not intend to fulfill. The way you dress, the way you speak, the signals you send — these things matter. You are not responsible for every thought someone else has, but you are responsible for what you intentionally provoke. A young woman who dresses and acts to arouse interest she has no intention of honoring is not being admired. She is being consumed. And she is training young men to see women as objects rather than people.

Gossip and mockery. When young women talk about young men behind their backs — mocking their awkwardness, laughing at their attempts, sharing private conversations for entertainment — they do real damage. Men have dignity too. Their feelings are real. Their embarrassment is real. The fact that culture tells you men do not care does not make it true.

Why This Matters

Here is why you should care about treating young men well, even when it seems like no one else does:

Because God commands it. The instruction to treat younger men as brothers "in all purity" is not a suggestion. It is a command from the apostle Paul, carried by the authority of Scripture. You do not get to decide that this does not apply to you because the culture has moved on.

Because you will reap what you sow. The young woman who uses people will find herself used. The one who plays games will find herself caught in someone else's game. The one who treats others as disposable will eventually be treated as disposable herself. This is not just karma — it is the way God designed the moral universe to work.

> *"Do not be deceived, God is not mocked; for whatever a man sows, this he will also reap."*
>
> — Galatians 6:7 (NASB)

Because your character is being formed right now. The habits you build in how you treat people do not disappear when you get married. The young woman who manipulates young men will become a wife who manipulates her husband. The one who craves attention from multiple sources will not suddenly be satisfied with one. What you practice now is what you will be later.

Because he is a person made in God's image. Every human being carries the image of God — the imago Dei. That includes the young man you find annoying, the one you think is beneath you, and the one whose attention you enjoy but do not value. He is not a tool for your use. He is a soul with eternal significance, and God sees how you treat him.

What It Looks Like to Treat Him Well

So what does it actually look like to treat young men the way Scripture calls you to?

Be honest. If you are not interested, say so — kindly, but clearly. Do not leave someone guessing because you enjoy the attention or because you are afraid of an awkward conversation. Honest rejection is kinder than dishonest hope.

Be modest. This is not about following a dress code or covering yourself in shame. It is about recognizing that your choices affect other people. Modesty is considering how your appearance and behavior impact those around you, and choosing not to deliberately provoke what should not be provoked.

Be respectful. Speak about young men the way you would want them to speak about you. Do not mock. Do not gossip. Do not share private information for entertainment. Guard their dignity the way you want your dignity guarded.

Be encouraging. Young men face pressures you may not fully understand. They are told to be strong but sensitive, leaders but not dominating, ambitious but not threatening. Many of them are struggling to figure out who they are supposed to be. A kind word, a genuine compliment, an acknowledgment of something they did well — these things matter more than you know.

Be protective, not predatory. Instead of asking "What can I get from him?" ask "What is best for him?" That question changes everything. It moves you from consumer to guardian, from user to friend.

A Word About Boundaries

Treating young men with respect does not mean you owe them anything. You do not owe anyone a date, a conversation, or your time. You are not required to be nice to someone who is treating you badly. You are allowed to say no, to walk away, to protect yourself.

The call to treat others well is not a call to let yourself be mistreated. If a young man pressures you, disrespects you, or makes you feel unsafe, you have every right to remove yourself from the situation. Purity includes protecting yourself, not just protecting others.

But — and this is important — the existence of bad young men does not give you permission to treat all young men badly. The fact that some of them may act like animals does not mean you should treat the rest of them like animals. Protect yourself where you need to, and show respect where respect is warranted.

Thinking Long-Term

Let me give you one more reason to take this seriously.

The young man you marry — if you marry — is out there right now. He is living his life, making his choices, becoming whoever he is going to be when you meet him.

And right now, young women are treating him a certain way.

Some of them may be using him. Playing games with his heart. Teaching him that women are not to be trusted, that their words do not mean what they say, that love is just another word for manipulation.

Or they may be building him up. Encouraging him. Showing him that women can be trustworthy, that kindness exists, that not everyone is playing games.

You have no control over what other young women do. But you have complete control over what kind of young woman you are.

And somewhere out there, right now, there is a young man whose future wife is interacting with him. The way she treats him is shaping who he will be when he meets her — when he meets you.

> *Treat every young man the way you want your future husband to be treated right now.*

> *He is somebody's son.*

> *Treat him like it.*

In all purity.

For Further Study

These passages speak to how we treat others — with honor, integrity, and care.

- 1 Timothy 5:1–2 — Treating others as family, in all purity
- Philippians 2:3–4 — Regarding others as more important than yourself

- Galatians 6:7–10 — Sowing and reaping; doing good to all

- Romans 12:9–18 — Love without hypocrisy; honoring one another

> *"Do nothing from selfishness or empty conceit, but with humility of mind regard one another as more important than yourselves; do not merely look out for your own personal interests, but also for the interests of others."*
>
> — Philippians 2:3–4 (NASB)

CHAPTER 9

What to Expect from a Young Man Who Fears God

Part Three: How You Walk With People

The last chapter talked about how you should treat the young men in your life.

This one is about how they should treat you.

Both chapters matter. But this one is going to ask something different of you. The last chapter asked you to examine your own heart — to look at the way you carry yourself around young men and to take responsibility for it. This chapter is going to ask you to look at them — clearly, honestly, without flattering yourself about what you are seeing.

Because here is the truth that nobody seems willing to tell young women anymore:

> *You are allowed to have standards. And the standards God gives you are not negotiable.*

You are going to hear, over and over, that you should not be too picky. That nobody is perfect. That you are going to have to compromise. That if you wait for a young man who actually meets the standards God lays out in His Word, you will wait forever.

That last one is a lie — and it is the kind of lie that has wrecked more young women's lives than almost any other.

You will not wait forever. But you may have to wait. And you definitely have to be willing to walk away from anything less than what God says you deserve.

What Scripture Actually Says About How He Should Treat You

Let me show you what the Bible says about how a young man who fears God will treat a young woman. This is not my opinion. This is not a list of preferences I made up. This is what is in the text.

Paul wrote to a young preacher named Timothy and told him how to treat the women in the church. Listen carefully:

> *"Do not sharply rebuke an older man, but rather appeal to him as a father, to the younger men as brothers, the older women as mothers, and the younger women as sisters, in all purity."*
> — 1 Timothy 5:1–2 (NASB)

This is the same verse the last chapter used. But notice now what it requires of the young man. He is to treat younger women as sisters. *In all purity.*

A brother does not use his sister. He does not pressure her. He does not flatter her to get something from her. He does not test her boundaries to see how far she will let him push. He protects her. He honors her. He treats her with the kind of respect a man gives to family.

If a young man cannot treat you the way he would treat his own sister, he is not treating you the way Scripture commands.

> *If he cannot treat you with the dignity he would give*
> *his own sister, he has already failed the test.*

Pure Hearts and Self-Control

Paul wrote to Timothy again — this time about Timothy's own life — and gave him instruction that applies to every young man:

> *"Now flee from youthful lusts and pursue righteousness, faith, love and peace, with those who call on the Lord from a pure heart."*
>
> — 2 Timothy 2:22 (NASB)

Flee. Not manage. Not balance. Flee.

A young man who fears God does not test how close he can get to sin. He runs the other way. He does not try to see how much he can get away with. He does not flirt with what God has told him to avoid.

Paul wrote to the church at Thessalonica with the same standard:

> *"For this is the will of God, your sanctification; that is, that you abstain from sexual immorality; that each of you know how to possess his own vessel in sanctification and honor, not in lustful passion, like the Gentiles who do not know God; and that no man transgress and defraud his brother in the matter because the Lord is the avenger in all these things, as we also told you before and solemnly warned you."*
>
> — 1 Thessalonians 4:3–7 (NASB)

Read that carefully. Sanctification and honor. Not lustful passion. And notice the warning: *no man transgress and defraud his brother in the matter.*

When a young man uses a young woman for his own desires, he is defrauding someone else. He is taking what does not belong to him. He is acting like the people who do not know God — and the Lord is the avenger of those things.

A young man who reads those verses and takes them seriously is going to treat you very, very differently from a young man who has never read them — or has read them and ignored them.

You are looking for the first kind. The second kind, no matter how charming, is dangerous to you.

> *The young man who fears God treats you with sanctification and honor — because he knows the Lord is watching.*

The Picture of a Husband

Look ahead with me for a moment. The Bible tells us what kind of man a husband is supposed to be — and even though you are not thinking about marriage right now, this matters. Because the young man you spend time with now is becoming the kind of man he will be when someone marries him. And the way he treats you now is preparing him to treat someone the same way later.

Paul wrote to the church at Ephesus:

*"Husbands, love your wives, just as Christ also loved the church
and gave Himself up for her, so that He might sanctify her,
having cleansed her by the washing of water with the word, that
He might present to Himself the church in all her glory, having no
spot or wrinkle or any such thing; but that she would be holy and
blameless. So husbands ought also to love their own wives as their
own bodies. He who loves his own wife loves himself; for no one ever
hated his own flesh, but nourishes and cherishes it, just as Christ
also does the church."*

— Ephesians 5:25–29 (NASB)

That is the standard. A husband loves his wife the way Christ loved
the church — sacrificially, completely, with the goal of her holiness,
not his own pleasure.

Peter, writing to husbands, said it just as plainly:

*"You husbands in the same way, live with your wives in an
understanding way, as with someone weaker, since she is a
woman; and show her honor as a fellow heir of the grace of life, so
that your prayers will not be hindered."*

— 1 Peter 3:7 (NASB)

Honor. Understanding. Recognition that she is a fellow heir of the
grace of life.

The young man who one day marries you should already be
practicing this. Not perfectly — nobody is perfect. But the direction
of his life should be toward this. You should be able to see, in the
way he treats you now, the kind of husband he will eventually
become.

If what you see is selfishness, pressure, dishonor, or pride — you are looking at the kind of husband he is going to be. Do not deceive yourself into thinking marriage will fix him.

> *How he treats you now is the rough draft of how he will treat you for the rest of his life.*

What Pursuit With Honor Looks Like

The Bible gives us examples of men who pursued women the right way. Let me show you two.

The first is Jacob. He fell in love with a young woman named Rachel — and her father, Laban, told Jacob he would have to work seven years for her. Seven years. No shortcut, no payment, no other way around it. Just patient labor for the woman he loved.

And here is what Genesis says about those seven years:

> *"So Jacob served seven years for Rachel and they seemed to him but a few days because of his love for her."*
> — Genesis 29:20 (NASB)

A few days. Seven years felt like a few days because he loved her.

That is what real love does. It waits. It works. It does not demand to take what it has not earned. It does not pressure for shortcuts. The young man who loves you the way Jacob loved Rachel will be patient — because patience is what love does.

The second example is Boaz, the kinsman-redeemer in Ruth's story. When Ruth came into his fields gleaning, Boaz noticed her — but watch what he did.

He spoke to her kindly (Ruth 2:8). He gave her his protection — telling his young men not to touch her (Ruth 2:9). He provided for her beyond what was required (Ruth 2:14–16). And when Ruth came to him alone at night, in vulnerability, asking him to be her redeemer — when he could have taken advantage of her — he did the opposite. He praised her character. He covered her. He told her to wait until morning.

> *"Now, my daughter, do not fear. I will do for you whatever you ask, for all my people in the city know that you are a woman of excellence."*
>
> — Ruth 3:11 (NASB)

He could have done what most men would have done. He did not. He honored her. He protected her. And he did things in the right way — through the proper channels, in front of witnesses, with no shortcuts.

That is what a young man who fears God looks like. He notices. He provides. He protects. He does not take. He waits. He honors.

Find one of those. Settle for nothing less.

> *Watch what he does when you are vulnerable. That is the test that reveals everything.*

What Scripture Names as Disgraceful

Now I have to talk to you about something hard.

The Bible does not pretend that all young men are good young men. It does not pretend that everyone who claims to follow God actually does. And it gives us — preserved for us, for thousands of years — the words of a young woman who was being treated in a way that no young woman should ever be treated.

Her name was Tamar. She was the daughter of King David. And she was being violated by her own half-brother — a man who should have protected her.

You can read the full account in 2 Samuel 13. It is a hard chapter. But what I want you to see is what Tamar said when it was happening:

> *"No, my brother, do not violate me, for such a thing is not done in Israel; do not do this disgraceful thing! As for me, where could I get rid of my reproach? And as for you, you will be like one of the fools in Israel."*
>
> — 2 Samuel 13:12–13 (NASB)

Read those words again. Tamar named what was happening. She did not minimize it. She did not pretend it was something other than what it was. She called it a *disgraceful thing*. And she named what her brother was becoming in that moment — *one of the fools in Israel.*

God preserved her words. He preserved them for thousands of years so that you, sitting where you are right now, would have a category and a vocabulary for what is being done to you when somebody is doing it.

When a young man pressures you to do what God has said no to — that is a disgraceful thing.

When a young man tries to take what is not his to take — that is a disgraceful thing.

When a young man treats you in a way that you know, in your gut, is wrong — even if you cannot fully articulate why — Scripture has already given you the word. That is a disgraceful thing. And the man doing it is a fool.

You are not required to be polite to a fool. You are not required to soften the language. You are not required to make excuses for him or to wonder if maybe you misunderstood. Tamar did not soften her language, and Scripture honored her by preserving every word.

If a young man is doing what Tamar's brother did — or pressuring toward it, or hinting at it, or testing you to see how far he can push — get away from him. Tell a trusted adult. Do not be alone with him. Do not give him another chance to wear you down.

This is not paranoia. This is wisdom.

> *Scripture itself has given you the vocabulary. What is being demanded of you is disgraceful. The man demanding it is a fool. You owe him no second chance.*

The Test That Tells the Truth

So how do you actually tell the difference between a young man who fears God and one who is just good at sounding like he does?

You watch him over time. And you look for fruit.

Paul wrote to the churches in Galatia and gave them a list — a checklist, really — of what the Spirit of God produces in a person's life:

"But the fruit of the Spirit is love, joy, peace, patience, kindness, goodness, faithfulness, gentleness, self-control; against such things there is no law."

— Galatians 5:22–23 (NASB)

Read that list slowly.

Love. Joy. Peace. Patience. Kindness. Goodness. Faithfulness. Gentleness. Self-control.

Those are not feelings. They are not moods. They are observable patterns in a person's life. You can see whether someone is patient or not. You can see whether someone is kind. You can see whether someone has self-control — particularly when nothing is going his way.

If you watch a young man's life — not just how he acts when he is trying to impress you, but how he acts when he is frustrated, tired, angry, or alone — and you do not see this fruit, then the Spirit of God is not at work in him. It is that simple.

A young man who claims to follow God but cannot control his temper does not have the Spirit's self-control.

A young man who is harsh with people who cannot do anything for him does not have the Spirit's kindness.

A young man who cannot wait — for anything, ever — does not have the Spirit's patience.

You do not need a degree in theology to read his life. You just need to pay attention. And you need to be honest with yourself about what you are seeing.

Watch the fruit. The Spirit of God produces patterns
you can see — and so does the absence of Him.

The Truth You Have to Hear

There is one more thing that has to be said, and it is the hardest thing in this chapter.

You cannot change him.

It does not matter how much you love him. It does not matter how much potential you see in him. It does not matter how convinced you are that under all of his selfishness or arrogance or pressure, there is a good young man waiting to come out — if only the right young woman will love him into it.

That is a story the world tells. It is not a story God tells.

Only God changes a person. Only God's Spirit produces the fruit we just talked about. You do not have that power. You were never meant to. And every young woman who has tried to be the redeemer of a young man who refused to be redeemed has paid for it — sometimes for the rest of her life.

If a young man is not walking with God now, you cannot walk him there. If he does not honor you now, your love will not teach him how. If he is cruel, careless, dishonest, or selfish now — when he should be at his best, when he is trying to win you — that is the floor of who he is, not the ceiling. He will not get better when he is comfortable. He will get worse.

A young woman who marries a young man hoping he will change is making a bargain that almost never works. The man you marry is, in nearly every case, the man you will be married to until one of you is buried.

So choose carefully. And do not flatter yourself about your power to fix what God alone can fix.

A Word About Walking Away

If you are reading this and realizing that the young man you are interested in — or the one already pursuing you — does not meet what Scripture describes, here is what you need to know:

Walking away is not failure. Walking away is wisdom.

You are not betraying him by stepping back. You are not being heartless. You are not being too picky. You are obeying God's Word, which has told you, in a hundred different places, what kind of man is worth your trust.

The young man who is right for you will not require you to lower your standards. He will rise to meet them — because he is already trying to meet God's.

Anyone who asks you to compromise what Scripture has told you to hold onto is not the right one. Not because he is not a nice person. Not because he does not have good qualities. Because the standard is not yours to lower.

Wait for the young man who already fears God. Watch his life. Look for the fruit. Pay attention to how he treats you when nothing is on the line. Pay attention to how he treats other people — his mother, his sisters, the cashier, the friend who cannot do anything for him.

That is the young man worth your time.

The standard is not negotiable. Wait for the one who already meets it.

You are allowed to have standards.

God Himself wrote them.

Settle for nothing less.

Pursue righteousness, faith, love and peace, with those who call on the Lord from a pure heart.

For Further Study

These are the passages this chapter was built from. Read them slowly, and let them settle.

- 1 Timothy 5:1–2 — Treating younger women as sisters, in all purity
- 2 Timothy 2:22 — Flee youthful lusts; pursue with a pure heart
- 1 Thessalonians 4:3–7 — Sanctification and honor, not lustful passion
- Ephesians 5:25–29 — How a husband is to love his wife
- 1 Peter 3:7 — Honor as a fellow heir of the grace of life
- Genesis 29:15–20 — Jacob's seven years for Rachel

- Ruth 2–4 — Boaz: noticing, providing, protecting, doing things the right way

- 2 Samuel 13:1–22 — Tamar's words; the disgraceful thing; the fool in Israel

- Galatians 5:22–23 — The fruit of the Spirit as a litmus test

> *"Now flee from youthful lusts and pursue righteousness, faith, love and peace, with those who call on the Lord from a pure heart."*
>
> — 2 Timothy 2:22 (NASB)

CHAPTER 10

The Friends You Choose Will Choose Your Future

Part Three: How You Walk With People

There is an old saying: show me your friends, and I will show you your future.

It sounds like something a parent would say to end an argument. But it is true. The people you spend your time with shape who you become — not in some vague, theoretical way, but in concrete, measurable ways. Their values seep into your values. Their habits become your habits. Their standards become the baseline against which you measure yourself.

This is not a mystery. It is how human beings work. We are social creatures, designed to be influenced by the people around us. That influence can pull you up or drag you down, but it is never neutral.

Scripture puts it plainly:

> *"One who walks with wise men will be wise, but the companion of fools will suffer harm."*
> — Proverbs 13:20 (NASB)

Notice what this proverb does not say. It does not say you might suffer harm. It does not say it is possible you could be negatively influenced. It says you will. The companion of fools will suffer harm. It is a certainty.

Ruth and Naomi

One of the most beautiful friendships in Scripture is between two women: Ruth and Naomi.

Their story begins in tragedy. Naomi was an Israelite woman who had moved with her husband and two sons to the land of Moab during a famine. While there, her sons married Moabite women — Orpah and Ruth. And then, over the course of about ten years, Naomi's husband died. Then both of her sons died. Three widows were left with nothing.

Naomi decided to return to Israel. She had heard that the famine was over, and she had nothing left in Moab. She told her daughters-in-law to go back to their own families, to find new husbands among their own people. It was the practical thing to do. It made sense.

Orpah, weeping, did exactly that. She kissed Naomi goodbye and went home.

But Ruth refused.

> *"Do not urge me to leave you or turn back from following you; for
> where you go, I will go, and where you lodge, I will lodge. Your
> people shall be my people, and your God, my God. Where you die,
> I will die, and there I will be buried. Thus may the Lord do to me,
> and worse, if anything but death parts you and me."*
> — Ruth 1:16–17 (NASB)

This is one of the most famous declarations of loyalty ever spoken. It is read at weddings, engraved on jewelry, quoted in poems. But it was not spoken by a bride to a groom. It was spoken by a young woman to her mother-in-law.

Ruth chose Naomi. She chose to leave her homeland, her people, her gods, and her future prospects — all to stay with a bitter, grieving older woman who had nothing to offer her. By every worldly calculation, it was a foolish decision.

But Ruth saw something the world could not measure. She saw a woman of faith. She saw the God of Israel, who was worth more than the gods of Moab. And she chose to bind her life to both.

> *Ruth's choice of friend determined the entire trajectory
> of her life.*

What Happened Next

If Ruth had gone back to Moab with Orpah, her story would have ended there. She would have been a footnote — a Moabite widow who made the sensible choice and disappeared into history.

Instead, she became one of the most significant women in the Bible.

Ruth went with Naomi to Bethlehem. There, she worked in the fields to provide for them both, gleaning grain left behind by the harvesters. Her hard work and her loyalty caught the attention of a man named Boaz — a relative of Naomi's late husband, a man of wealth and character.

Boaz married Ruth. They had a son named Obed. Obed had a son named Jesse. And Jesse had a son named David — the king of Israel, the man after God's own heart.

And from David's line came Jesus.

Ruth, the Moabite widow who chose to follow Naomi, is listed in the genealogy of Christ. Her loyalty to a godly friend placed her in the lineage of the Savior of the world.

That is what can happen when you choose your friends wisely.

The Friends Who Pull You Down

Not all friendships lead to blessing.

Some friendships are easy because they ask nothing of you. They let you stay exactly as you are — or worse, they encourage you to become less than you could be. They make the wrong things feel normal. They celebrate what should be questioned. They pull you away from God, away from wisdom, away from the future you were made for.

You probably know which friendships these are. You feel it after you spend time with certain people — the vague sense that you have been diminished, that you laughed at things you should not have laughed at, that you compromised something without quite realizing it.

These friendships are dangerous precisely because they do not feel dangerous. They feel fun. They feel comfortable. They feel like freedom. But they are slowly shaping you into someone you did not choose to become.

> *"Do not be deceived: 'Bad company corrupts good morals.'"*
> — 1 Corinthians 15:33 (NASB)

Paul wrote those words to a church, but they apply to everyone. Bad company corrupts good morals. Not might corrupt. Does corrupt. The influence is real, and it is inevitable.

This does not mean you cannot be kind to everyone. It does not mean you should be rude to people who are not Christians or who do not share your values. Jesus ate with sinners. He spoke to outcasts. He loved people who were far from God.

But there is a difference between loving someone and choosing them as your closest companion. You can be kind to anyone. You cannot walk closely with everyone. The people you let into your inner circle — the ones who influence your thoughts, your habits, and your heart — those choices matter.

The Friends Who Build You Up

The right friendships do the opposite. They call you higher. They make you want to be better. They speak truth when you need to hear it and encourage you when you are ready to give up.

A true friend does not just tell you what you want to hear.

"Faithful are the wounds of a friend, but deceitful are the kisses of an enemy."
— Proverbs 27:6 (NASB)

A friend who only flatters you is not really a friend. A friend who tells you the truth — even when it is uncomfortable, even when it wounds — is giving you a gift. She sees something you cannot see and cares enough to say it.

The right friends share your faith. This does not mean you can only be friends with Christians, but it means your closest friends — the ones who shape you most — should be people who are walking in the same direction. You cannot follow Christ closely while your closest companions are walking the other way.

"Iron sharpens iron, so one person sharpens another."
— Proverbs 27:17 (NASB)

Iron sharpens iron. Not iron and cotton. Not iron and water. It takes something equally strong to sharpen you. Weak friendships produce weak people. Strong friendships — built on shared faith, mutual respect, and honest love — produce women of strength and dignity.

Choosing Wisely

So how do you choose friends wisely? Here are some questions to ask yourself:

Does this person share my faith? Again, this does not mean you cannot have non-Christian friends. But your closest companions should be people who love God and are trying to follow Him. If the person who knows you best and influences you most does not share your deepest convictions, you are building on an unstable foundation.

Do I become a better person when I am around her? After spending time with this friend, do you feel encouraged, challenged, built up? Or do you feel empty, compromised, a little less yourself? Your gut often knows the answer even when your mind makes excuses.

Does she tell me the truth? A friend who only agrees with you is not helping you grow. Look for friends who love you enough to say hard things — and who can receive hard things when you say them back.

Is she going somewhere? Not in terms of career or worldly success, but in terms of character. Is she growing? Is she becoming more like Christ? Or is she stagnant, drifting, comfortable with staying the same? The direction your friend is heading is the direction you will be pulled.

Would I want to be like her in ten years? This is the most clarifying question of all. Look at your friend's trajectory. If she keeps going the way she is going, do you want to be where she ends up? Because if you stay close to her, you probably will be.

Be the Friend Worth Choosing

There is one more thing to say about friendship, and it is this: the standard you apply to others should be the standard you apply to yourself.

Do you want friends who are faithful? Be faithful.

Do you want friends who speak truth? Speak truth.

Do you want friends who encourage you and build you up? Be that kind of friend to others.

Ruth was not just looking for a good friend. She was being a good friend. Her loyalty to Naomi was extraordinary. Her commitment was total. She gave before she received. She served before she was served.

If you want to attract friends of depth and character, become a person of depth and character. If you want to be surrounded by women who sharpen you, become a woman who sharpens others.

> *The best way to find the right friends is to become the right friend.*

> *The friends you choose will choose your future.*

> *Choose wisely.*

Walk with the wise.

For Further Study

Read Ruth's story in full. It is only four chapters — one of the shortest books in the Bible — and one of the most beautiful.

- Ruth 1–4 — The complete story of Ruth and Naomi

- Proverbs 13:20 — Walking with the wise

- Proverbs 27:5–6, 17 — Faithful wounds, iron sharpening iron

• 1 Corinthians 15:33 — Bad company corrupts good morals

> *"Do not urge me to leave you or turn back from following you; for where you go, I will go, and where you lodge, I will lodge. Your people shall be my people, and your God, my God."*
>
> — Ruth 1:16 (NASB)

CHAPTER 11

Honor Your Father and Mother (Even When It's Hard)

Part Three: How You Walk With People

(Even When It's Hard)

This may be the hardest chapter in this book.

Not because the command is complicated. It is one of the clearest things God ever said. And not because you do not understand it — you do. It is hard because your situation may be complicated, even when the command is not.

Some of you reading this have wonderful parents. They are present, they are trying, they love you the best way they know how. If that is you, do not skip this chapter. You need it — because it is easy to take good parents for granted until the day you no longer have them.

And some of you are reading this with a knot in your stomach. Because when someone says "honor your father and mother," what comes to mind is not a warm feeling. Maybe your father left. Maybe your mother is harsh. Maybe one of your parents struggles with something that has turned your home into something unpredictable. Maybe they are not terrible people — just difficult ones, in ways that wear you down day after day.

This chapter is for all of you. Because the command does not change based on your circumstances.

Scripture puts it simply:

> *"Children, obey your parents in the Lord, for this is right. Honor your father and mother (which is the first commandment with a promise), so that it may be well with you, and that you may live long on the earth."*
>
> — Ephesians 6:1–3 (NASB)

Paul is quoting from the Ten Commandments — from Exodus 20:12. But notice that he does not present it as an outdated relic of the Old Law. He repeats it under the New Covenant, to the church at Ephesus, and he reinforces it: this is the first commandment with a promise.

God does not attach promises to throwaway instructions. When He says that honoring your parents is connected to things going well with you, He means it.

> *This is not a suggestion. It is a command — and it comes with a promise attached.*

The First Commandment with a Promise

Think about what Paul is saying. Of all the commandments God gave, this is the first one that comes with a specific promise of blessing. Not "do not steal." Not "do not lie." Honor your father and mother — that is the one God chose to reinforce with a promise.

Why?

Because God knows what this costs. He knows that parents are imperfect. He knew it when He gave the command. He was not speaking to children of perfect parents — those do not exist. He was speaking to every child. And He attached a promise to it because He knew that obedience in this area would require something of you.

The original command was given to Israel: "Honor your father and your mother, that your days may be prolonged in the land which the LORD your God gives you" (Exodus 20:12, NASB). Paul picks it up and applies it to Christians. The principle carries forward. The command did not expire at the cross. It was confirmed.

What Does "Honor" Actually Mean?

This is where many people get confused — and where being honest with the text matters.

The word Paul uses in Ephesians 6:2 is the Greek word timao. It means to value, to regard as weighty, to treat as significant. It carries the idea of assigning worth to someone.

But notice something important. Paul uses two different words in this passage. In verse 1, he says "obey." In verse 2, he says "honor." These are not the same thing.

Obedience is about compliance — doing what you are told. It is the word Paul uses for children who are still under their parents' authority. "Children, obey your parents in the Lord, for this is right."

Honor is broader and deeper. It is about how you regard someone, how you speak about them, how you treat them. And unlike obedience, honor has no expiration date. You may outgrow the season of obedience to your parents. You will never outgrow the command to honor them.

A grown woman does not obey her mother the way a ten-year-old does. But a grown woman should still honor her mother — in how she speaks to her, how she speaks about her, how she treats her, and how she regards her in her heart.

> *Obedience has a season. Honor is for life.*

When It Is Easy

If you have parents who love you, who are present, who are trying to raise you well — even imperfectly — you have been given a gift. Do not miss it.

It is easy when you are young to see only your parents' flaws. They embarrass you. They do not understand your world. They say the wrong things in front of your friends. They hold you to standards that feel outdated or unfair.

Can I tell you something? You will not always have them.

The day will come — sooner than you think — when you would give almost anything to hear your mother tell you what to do one more time. When the house that felt so suffocating will be the place you miss most. When the voice that annoyed you will be the voice you long to hear again.

Do not wait until then to honor them.

Honor them now by listening — really listening — even when you think they are wrong. Honor them by speaking respectfully, even when you are frustrated. Honor them by obeying while you are under their roof, even when you disagree. Honor them by being the kind of daughter they do not have to worry about when they lay their heads down at night.

The writer of Proverbs says it this way:

> *"Listen to your father who begot you, and do not despise your mother when she is old."*
> — Proverbs 23:22 (NASB)

And a few verses later:

> *"Let your father and your mother be glad, and let her who bore you rejoice."*
> — Proverbs 23:25 (NASB)

You have the power to bring your parents gladness or grief. Every day, in how you treat them, you are choosing one or the other.

When It Is Hard

Now the harder conversation.

Some of you do not have the parents described above. Your father is absent — physically, emotionally, or both. Your mother is controlling, or volatile, or battling something that makes your home feel unsafe. Maybe your parents are divorced and you are caught in the middle of two worlds that do not fit together. Maybe the person who was supposed to protect you is the one who has hurt you.

This chapter does not pretend those realities do not exist. And it will not insult you by offering easy answers to hard situations.

But here is what it will say: the command still stands.

Honor your father and mother — even when it is hard.

That probably feels unfair. And I understand why. But before you push back, let me explain what honor does not mean in these situations.

Honor does not mean pretending everything is fine when it is not. Honor does not mean accepting mistreatment and calling it love. Honor does not mean staying silent when speaking up would protect you or someone else. Honor does not mean enabling a parent's sin by covering for them, lying for them, or allowing them to destroy themselves and everyone around them without consequence.

Honor does not require you to be a doormat. God never asked that of anyone.

But honor does mean refusing to return evil for evil. Paul wrote to the Romans:

"Never pay back evil for evil to anyone."
— Romans 12:17 (NASB)

That is not just advice for dealing with strangers. It applies to your parents too. When they are harsh, you do not have to be harsh in return. When they are unkind, you do not have to match their unkindness. You can be honest about what they have done — to a trusted adult, to a counselor, to God — without tearing them apart publicly, without savaging their name, without returning wound for wound.

That is honor in a hard place. And it is one of the bravest things a young woman can do.

What Honor Looks Like in Hard Places

Let me be specific, because vague advice does not help anyone.

If your parent is difficult but not dangerous — if they are frustrating, overbearing, harsh with their words, or simply hard to be around — honor looks like this: speaking respectfully even when they do not. Choosing patience when your instinct is to fight back. Praying for them — not performatively, but sincerely. Not gossiping about them to your friends. Trying, genuinely trying, to see the burdens they carry that you may not fully understand yet.

If your parent is dangerous — if there is abuse, if addiction has created an unsafe home, if their behavior puts you or others at genuine risk — honor does not mean staying in harm's way. Protecting yourself is not dishonoring your parent. Telling a trusted adult — a teacher, a counselor, an elder, a grandparent — is not betrayal. It is wisdom. Sometimes it is the most honoring thing you can do, because it says: this situation is not right, and I believe we both deserve better than this.

Even in the hardest situations, honor means you do not let their failures define who you become. You can choose to be kind even though someone was unkind to you. You can choose to be present even though someone was absent from your life. You can choose to be faithful even though someone broke faith with you.

> *You are not responsible for what your parents did. You are responsible for who you become.*

Jesus and His Mother

Even Jesus honored His mother.

Think about that for a moment. The Son of God — the One through whom all things were created — submitted Himself to the authority of a human mother and an earthly father. Luke records that as a boy, Jesus "continued in subjection to them" (Luke 2:51, NASB). The Creator of the universe obeyed Mary and Joseph.

And at the very end of His life, while He was dying on the cross, in unimaginable agony, He looked down and saw His mother standing there. And even then — even in that moment — He thought of her. He turned to the disciple He loved and said:

"Woman, behold, your son!"

And then He said to the disciple:

"Behold, your mother!"
— John 19:26–27 (NASB)

He made sure she would be cared for. He made sure she would not be alone. With some of His final words, He honored His mother.

If Jesus — in the worst moment any human being has ever endured — still thought of His mother's welfare, then you and I have no ground to treat ours with carelessness.

If the Son of God honored His mother, so can you.

The Harder Truth

Here is something nobody wants to say out loud, but you need to hear it: your parents will fail you.

That is not cynicism. It is reality. Every human parent is exactly that — human. Fallen, limited, carrying their own wounds, making mistakes they may not even see. Even the best parents will disappoint you at some point. Even the most loving mother will say the wrong thing at the wrong time. Even the most devoted father will miss something that mattered to you deeply.

This is not a reason to withhold honor. It is a reason to understand what honor actually costs — and where your deepest need for a perfect Parent is truly met.

Jesus taught His disciples to pray: "Our Father who is in heaven" (Matthew 6:9, NASB). God is the Father who never leaves. The Father who never disappoints. The Father whose love is not moody, not distracted, not conditional. Every earthly parent is an imperfect reflection of that perfect Father.

When your earthly parents fall short — and they will — the answer is not bitterness. The answer is to take your unmet needs to the Father who can actually meet them, and to extend grace to the parents who could not.

That grace does not excuse sin. It does not minimize real harm. But it keeps your heart from becoming hard. And a hard heart will cost you far more than a difficult parent ever could.

> *"See to it that no one comes short of the grace of God; that no root of bitterness springing up causes trouble, and by it many be defiled."*
> — Hebrews 12:15 (NASB)

Bitterness is a poison you drink hoping the other person will suffer. It does not work. It never has. The only person it destroys is you.

A Word About Forgiveness

You may need to forgive your parents. Not because what they did was acceptable — but because carrying it will break you.

Forgiveness is not saying "it did not matter." It is saying "it will not own me." It is not a feeling you wait for. It is a decision you make — one you may have to make over and over again before your heart catches up with your will.

And you can forgive someone while still maintaining boundaries. You can forgive and still not trust someone with things they have proven they cannot handle. Forgiveness and trust are not the same thing. Forgiveness is commanded. Trust is earned.

If this is where you are — if you are carrying something heavy from a parent who wounded you — know that you are not alone. And know that God does not ask you to carry it by yourself. Take it to Him. Tell Him the honest truth about what happened. He already knows, and He is not afraid of your pain.

> *Honor your father and your mother.*

> *Not because they are perfect. Not because they earned it. Not because it is easy.*

Obey the command. Trust the promise.

For Further Study

This is one of the few commands repeated from the Old Testament
into the New. Read it carefully in both places.

- Exodus 20:12 — The original command with the promise

- Ephesians 6:1–3 — Paul's restatement to Christians

- Proverbs 23:22–25 — A father's instruction and a mother's
  gladness

- Luke 2:51 — Jesus in subjection to His parents

- John 19:26–27 — Jesus honoring His mother from the cross

- Romans 12:17–21 — Responding to evil with good

- Hebrews 12:14–15 — The warning against bitterness

*"Honor your father and mother
(which is the first commandment with
a promise), so that it may be well with
you, and that you may live long on the
earth."*

— Ephesians 6:2–3 (NASB)

CHAPTER 12

Work Like It Matters Because It Does

Part Four: How You Build a Life

Nobody dreams about work.

When you were little and someone asked what you wanted to be when you grew up, you were not dreaming about alarm clocks and deadlines and long hours on your feet. You were dreaming about the thing itself — the stage, the classroom, the adventure. Nobody dreams about the grind. Everybody wants the destination without the road.

But here is what nobody tells you when you are young: the road is the point.

How you work — not just what you work at, but how you show up, how much of yourself you bring to it, how you handle the parts that are boring or thankless or invisible — that reveals more about your character than almost anything else in your life. Your work is not just what you do. It is who you are becoming while you do it.

And God has something very specific to say about it.

> *"Whatever you do, do your work heartily, as for the Lord rather than for men; knowing that from the Lord you will receive the reward of the inheritance. It is the Lord Christ whom you serve."*
>
> — Colossians 3:23–24 (NASB)

Paul is writing to the church at Colossae, and his instruction could not be more clear. Whatever you do — not just the impressive things, not just the things people notice, but *whatever you do* — do it heartily. The word in Greek is *ek psychēs* — from the soul. Work with your whole self. And do it as for the Lord, not for men.

This changes everything. If your work is ultimately for God, then no task is beneath you. No job is meaningless. No assignment is wasted. The audience is not your boss, your teacher, or your social media followers. The audience is God.

> *When you work for the Lord, every task has dignity —*
> *because every task is an act of worship.*

Work Is Not a Curse

Before we go any further, you need to understand something the world gets wrong: work is not a punishment.

Many people treat work as if it were part of the curse — as if human beings were designed for leisure and work was inflicted on us because of sin. That is not what the Bible says.

Go back to the very beginning. Before the fall, before sin entered the world, before anything went wrong — God gave Adam work to do.

> *"Then the LORD God took the man and put him into the garden*
> *of Eden to cultivate it and keep it."*
> — Genesis 2:15 (NASB)

Work existed in paradise. It was part of God's original design for human beings — not as a burden, but as a purpose. Adam was not placed in the garden to sit and watch things grow. He was placed there to cultivate and keep it. To tend it. To do something with it.

Sin did not create work. Sin made work harder. The ground would now produce thorns and thistles (Genesis 3:17–18). The labor would now involve sweat and frustration. But work itself was there from the beginning — and it was good.

This matters because if you think work is a curse, you will spend your life trying to avoid it. But if you understand that work is part of how God designed you to function, you will approach it completely differently. You were made to do something meaningful with your hands, your mind, and your time.

> *Work is not what happened because of the fall. Work is what God gave you before the fall.*

The Woman of Proverbs 31

There is one passage in Scripture that gives us the most detailed portrait of a woman of excellence. It is Proverbs 31:10–31 — and it has been misunderstood almost as often as it has been quoted.

Some women hear "Proverbs 31" and feel exhausted before they even open the text. They have been told it is an impossible standard — a superwoman checklist that no real person could live up to. Others have dismissed it as outdated, a relic of a culture that no longer exists.

Both reactions miss the point.

Proverbs 31 is not a checklist. It is a portrait. It was written as an acrostic poem — each verse beginning with a successive letter of the Hebrew alphabet — and it paints a picture of what a woman of noble character looks like in the full expression of her life. It is not a to-do list for tomorrow morning. It is a vision of a life well lived.

And the first thing you notice when you actually read it is this: this woman works.

She works hard. She works smart. She works with purpose.

"She looks for wool and flax and works with her hands in delight" (Proverbs 31:13, NASB). "She is like merchant ships; she brings her food from afar" (Proverbs 31:14, NASB). "She rises also while it is still night and gives food to her household and portions to her maidens" (Proverbs 31:15, NASB). "She considers a field and buys it; from her earnings she plants a vineyard" (Proverbs 31:16, NASB). "She senses that her gain is good; her lamp does not go out at night" (Proverbs 31:18, NASB).

This is not a passive woman waiting for someone else to provide for her. This is a woman who evaluates, invests, produces, manages, and creates. She runs a household, manages workers, makes business decisions, and provides for people who depend on her. She does it with excellence, and she does it with delight — not resentment.

But here is what makes this portrait truly remarkable. After all the descriptions of her work, her business sense, and her industry, Proverbs tells us what actually defines her:

> *"Strength and dignity are her clothing, and she smiles at the future. She opens her mouth in wisdom, and the teaching of kindness is on her tongue."*
>
> — Proverbs 31:25–26 (NASB)

Her clothing is not her wardrobe. It is strength and dignity. Her identity is not built on what she produces — it is built on who she is. She smiles at the future because she has built something solid beneath her. Her work flows from her character, not the other way around.

And the passage closes with this:

> *"Charm is deceitful and beauty is vain, but a woman who fears the LORD, she shall be praised. Give her the product of her hands, and let her works praise her in the gates."*
>
> — Proverbs 31:30–31 (NASB)

The world says charm and beauty are what matter. God says they are deceitful and vain. What matters is the fear of the Lord — and the work that flows from it. *Let her works praise her.* Not her appearance. Not her following. Not her brand. Her works.

> *The Proverbs 31 woman is not an impossible standard. She is a woman who fears God and works like it matters.*

Lydia: A Woman Who Worked and Served

Proverbs 31 gives us the portrait. The book of Acts gives us a real woman who lived it.

Her name was Lydia, and she was a seller of purple fabrics from the city of Thyatira. We meet her in Acts 16, when Paul arrived in the city of Philippi on his second missionary journey.

Purple fabric was a luxury good in the ancient world. The dye was expensive, the process was laborious, and the customers were wealthy. Lydia was not running a small market stall. She was a businesswoman — and a successful one.

But what matters most about Lydia is not her business. It is what she did with it.

> *"A woman named Lydia, from the city of Thyatira, a seller of purple fabrics, a worshiper of God, was listening; and the Lord opened her heart to respond to the things spoken by Paul. And when she and her household had been baptized, she urged us, saying, 'If you have judged me to be faithful to the Lord, come into my house and stay.' And she prevailed upon us."*
> — Acts 16:14–15 (NASB)

Notice what happened. Lydia heard the gospel, responded to it, was baptized — and immediately opened her home. She took her resources, her success, and her household, and she put them all in service to the Lord and to the church.

And this was not a one-time gesture. Later in the same chapter, after Paul and Silas had been beaten and imprisoned and miraculously released, Luke tells us where they went: "They went out of the prison and entered the house of Lydia, and when they saw the brethren, they encouraged them and departed" (Acts 16:40, NASB).

The brethren were gathering at Lydia's house. Her home had become a meeting place for the church. Her work had funded it. Her hospitality had opened it. Her faith had made it possible.

Lydia did not separate her work from her faith. She used one to serve the other. She worked hard in her trade, and she worked just as hard for the Lord.

> *Lydia's work gave her the means. Her faith gave her the purpose. She used both.*

The Problem with Laziness

Scripture has nothing good to say about laziness. Nothing.

The book of Proverbs is especially blunt:

> *"How long will you lie down, O sluggard? When will you arise from your sleep? A little sleep, a little slumber, a little folding of the hands to rest — your poverty will come in like a vagabond and your need like an armed man."*

— Proverbs 6:9–11 (NASB)

This is not gentle advice. It is a warning. Laziness leads somewhere — and that somewhere is poverty, dependence, and regret. A little sleep. A little slumber. A little folding of the hands. It does not feel like a catastrophic decision in the moment. It feels like rest. But it adds up.

The culture around you will not help with this. The world is full of messages that tell you rest is resistance, that ambition is toxic, that you deserve to take it easy. And while rest is genuinely important — God Himself rested on the seventh day — there is a difference between rest and laziness. Rest is what you earn after working hard. Laziness is what you choose instead of working at all.

Paul was direct with the Thessalonians on this point:

> *"For even when we were with you, we used to give you this order: if anyone is not willing to work, then he is not to eat, either."*
>
> — 2 Thessalonians 3:10 (NASB)

That sounds harsh to modern ears. But Paul was addressing a real problem in the church — people who had stopped working and were living off the generosity of others while contributing nothing. He called it what it was: disorder. And he told the church not to enable it.

You do not want to be the woman who expects others to carry what she is able to carry herself. You do not want to be the woman who waits for someone else to build the life she should be building. That is not strength. That is not dignity. That is something less than what God made you for.

> *Laziness does not look like a disaster until you look up one day and realize what it has cost you.*

What Excellent Work Looks Like

So what does it actually look like to work with excellence?

It starts with the small things. The homework you finish with care instead of rushing through. The job you show up to on time, every time, whether anyone notices or not. The task you complete thoroughly instead of cutting corners. The commitment you keep even when you no longer feel like it.

Excellence is not about being the best. It is about giving your best. There is a difference. Being the best is a comparison — it depends on who is standing next to you. Giving your best is a choice — it depends only on you and on the God you are working for.

Here is a practical test: would you be comfortable if Jesus were standing over your shoulder watching you do this? Not because He is looking for reasons to condemn you — but because He is the one you are actually working for. If you would be embarrassed by the effort you are giving, that tells you something.

Excellence also means faithfulness in the things nobody sees. Jesus said it plainly:

> *"He who is faithful in a very little thing is faithful also in much; and he who is unrighteous in a very little thing is unrighteous also in much."*
>
> — Luke 16:10 (NASB)

The way you handle small responsibilities is the way you will handle large ones. If you cannot be faithful with a homework assignment, why would God — or anyone else — trust you with something bigger? Faithfulness in small things is not a stepping stone. It is the test.

> *Excellence is not about being the best. It is about giving your best — every time, whether anyone sees it or not.*

Work as Witness

There is one more thing about work that you need to understand, and it may be the most important: how you work is a witness.

People are watching you. Not because you are famous, but because you are visible. Your coworkers, your classmates, your teachers, your neighbors — they all see how you carry yourself. And when they know you are a Christian, they are watching even more closely.

Paul told Titus to teach the younger believers to be models of good deeds — and he gave a reason:

> *"In all things show yourself to be an example of good deeds, with purity in doctrine, dignified, sound in speech which is beyond reproach, so that the opponent will be put to shame, having nothing bad to say about us."*
> — Titus 2:7–8 (NASB)

Your work ethic is a testimony. When you show up and do your job with excellence, with honesty, with kindness toward the people around you — that says something about the God you serve. When you cut corners, complain constantly, do the minimum, and treat your responsibilities with contempt — that says something too.

You may never stand behind a pulpit. You may never teach a Bible class. But every day, in how you work, you are preaching a sermon that the people around you can see. Make it one worth hearing.

> *Your work is a sermon the people around you read every day. Make it worth reading.*

> *Work like it matters. Because it does.*

> *Work heartily. Work honestly. Work as for the Lord.*

> *Let your works praise you in the gates.*

Whatever you do, do it from the soul.

For Further Study

The Bible has far more to say about work than most people realize. Start here.

- Colossians 3:23–24 — Work heartily, as for the Lord

- Proverbs 31:10–31 — The portrait of a woman of noble character

- Acts 16:14–15, 40 — Lydia: a businesswoman who served the church

- Genesis 2:15 — Work before the fall

- Proverbs 6:6–11 — The warning against laziness

- 2 Thessalonians 3:10 — If anyone is not willing to work

- Luke 16:10 — Faithful in little, faithful in much

- Titus 2:7–8 — Work as witness

"Whatever you do, do your work heartily, as for the Lord rather than for men; knowing that from the Lord you will receive the reward of the inheritance. It is the Lord Christ whom you serve."

— Colossians 3:23–24 (NASB)

CHAPTER 13

Money Will Test Your Character

Part Four: How You Build a Life

Nobody ever thinks money will be their problem.

When you are young, money feels like a solution — the answer to every limitation you currently face. If you just had more of it, you could do what you wanted, go where you wanted, be who you wanted. Money looks like freedom.

But money is not freedom. Money is a test.

It tests what you love. It tests what you trust. It tests what you are willing to do — and what you are willing to become — in order to get it and keep it. Money does not change your character. It reveals it. And it will reveal yours sooner than you think.

Jesus said more about money than He said about almost any other subject. That should tell you something. He did not talk about it because He was interested in your financial planning. He talked about it because He knew what it would do to your heart if you were not careful.

> *"Do not store up for yourselves treasures on earth, where moth and rust destroy, and where thieves break in and steal. But store up for yourselves treasures in heaven, where neither moth nor rust destroys, and where thieves do not break in or steal; for where your treasure is, there your heart will be also."*
>
> — Matthew 6:19–21 (NASB)

That last line is the one that matters most. Where your treasure is, there your heart will be also. Jesus is not giving financial advice. He is diagnosing a spiritual condition. What you spend your money on tells the truth about what you love — even when your mouth says something different.

> *Money does not change who you are. It reveals who you are.*

The Love of Money

Paul wrote one of the most misquoted verses in the entire Bible:

> *"For the love of money is a root of all sorts of evil, and some by longing for it have wandered away from the faith and pierced themselves with many griefs."*
>
> — 1 Timothy 6:10 (NASB)

Notice what the text actually says. It does not say money is the root of all evil. Money is a tool. It is morally neutral. A hammer can build a house or break a window — the hammer does not decide. Money is the same way. It can fund a missionary, feed the hungry, support a church, and provide for a family. Or it can destroy every one of those things.

The problem is not money. The problem is the *love* of money. It is the longing for it. The craving. The willingness to let it sit on the throne of your heart where only God belongs.

And notice what Paul says happens when someone gives in to that love: they wander away from the faith. They pierce themselves with many griefs. The love of money does not lead to satisfaction. It leads to wandering and grief. It promises fulfillment and delivers emptiness.

You will meet people in your life who have a great deal of money and very little peace. You will meet others who have almost nothing and possess a joy that money cannot explain. The difference is never the amount in the account. The difference is what sits on the throne.

> *Money is not the problem. Loving it is.*

Women Who Used What They Had

Scripture gives us real examples of women who had means and used them well — not for their own comfort, but for the work of the Lord.

We have already met Lydia — the seller of purple fabrics who opened her home to the apostles and to the church at Philippi (Acts 16:14–15, 40). Her business funded her faithfulness. She did not hoard what she had earned. She put it to work for the kingdom.

But Lydia was not the only one.

Luke tells us something remarkable about the women who followed Jesus during His earthly ministry:

Read that carefully. Jesus and the twelve were traveling from city to city, preaching the kingdom of God. And the text says there were women — named women — who were contributing to their support out of their private means.

Joanna was the wife of Chuza, who was Herod's steward. This was not a woman of modest means. Her husband managed the finances of the royal household. She had access to wealth that most people in first-century Palestine could not imagine. And she used it — not to build a more comfortable life for herself, but to support the ministry of Jesus Christ.

Mary Magdalene is named. Susanna is named. And then Luke adds, "and many others." This was not one generous woman. It was a pattern — women who had resources and chose to pour them into the work of the Lord.

These women understood something that many people never learn: what you have is not really yours. It was given to you. And the best thing you can do with it is give it back.

The Widow's Two Coins

There is another woman in Scripture whose story about money is even more striking — and she is never named.

> *"And He sat down opposite the treasury, and began observing how the people were putting money into the treasury; and many rich people were putting in large sums. A poor widow came and put in two small copper coins, which amount to a cent. Calling His disciples to Him, He said to them, 'Truly I say to you, this poor widow put in more than all the contributors to the treasury; for they all put in out of their surplus, but she, out of her poverty, put in all she owned, all she had to live on.'"*
>
> — Mark 12:41–44 (NASB)

Jesus was watching the treasury — not the amounts going in, but *how* people were giving. The rich put in large sums, and nobody questioned their generosity. But it was the widow — the woman with two small copper coins — who caught His attention.

Why? Because she gave everything. The rich gave out of their surplus. She gave out of her poverty. They gave what they would never miss. She gave what she could not afford to lose.

Jesus did not measure generosity by the amount. He measured it by the cost.

This matters for you right now, even if you do not have much. You do not need to be wealthy to be generous. Generosity is not about the size of the gift. It is about the size of the sacrifice. The question is not "how much did you give?" The question is "what did it cost you?"

> *God does not measure your generosity by what you gave. He measures it by what you kept.*

Contentment: The War You Will Fight

If money is a test, contentment is how you pass it.

The world will spend your entire life trying to convince you that you do not have enough. That is not an accident. It is a business model. Every advertisement, every influencer, every "must-have" product is designed to create a feeling of lack — to make you believe that whatever you have right now is not sufficient.

It is a lie. And if you believe it, you will spend your life chasing something that keeps moving.

Paul understood this. He had lived with abundance and he had lived with nothing, and he said something extraordinary:

> *"Not that I speak from want, for I have learned to be content in whatever circumstances I am. I know how to get along with humble means, and I also know how to live in prosperity; in any and every circumstance I have learned the secret of being filled and going hungry, both of having abundance and suffering need. I can do all things through Him who strengthens me."*
>
> — Philippians 4:11–13 (NASB)

Notice that contentment was something Paul *learned.* It did not come naturally to him any more than it comes naturally to you. It was a discipline — a practice — something he had to work at. And notice where his contentment came from: not from having enough money, but from Christ who strengthened him.

That last verse — "I can do all things through Him who strengthens me" — is one of the most misused verses in the Bible. People put it on coffee cups and gym shirts as if Paul were talking about winning games or getting promotions. He was not. He was talking about contentment. He was saying: through Christ, I can be content whether I have much or little. That is the "all things" he is talking about.

Contentment is not about having everything you want. It is about wanting what you have — because you trust the God who gave it to you.

The writer of Hebrews puts it plainly:

> *"Make sure that your character is free from the love of money, being content with what you have; for He Himself has said, 'I will never desert you, nor will I ever forsake you.'"*
>
> — Hebrews 13:5 (NASB)

The cure for the love of money is not poverty. It is the promise of God's presence. He will never leave you. He will never forsake you. When you believe that — really believe it — the grip that money has on your heart begins to loosen.

> *Contentment is not having everything you want. It is trusting the God who gives you what you need.*

Generosity: The Antidote

If the love of money is a disease, generosity is the cure.

There is something that happens inside you when you give. Not because giving earns you anything with God — it does not. Salvation is a gift, not a transaction. But giving breaks the power that money wants to hold over your heart. When you give freely, you declare that your security is not in the money. It is in God.

Paul encouraged the church at Corinth with this principle:

> *"Now this I say, he who sows sparingly will also reap sparingly, and he who sows bountifully will also reap bountifully. Each one must do just as he has purposed in his heart, not grudgingly or under compulsion, for God loves a cheerful giver."*
>
> — 2 Corinthians 9:6–7 (NASB)

A cheerful giver. Not a reluctant giver. Not someone who gives because they feel guilty or pressured. Someone who gives because they have decided in their heart that this is what they want to do with what God has given them.

Start now. You do not have to wait until you are wealthy to practice generosity. Give to the church. Give to someone in need. Give your time, your resources, your attention to people who cannot repay you. Build the muscle now — because if you do not learn to give when you have little, you will not give when you have much.

> *If you will not give when you have little, you will not give when you have much.*

A Few Practical Words

This chapter would not be complete without some plain talk about how to handle money well while you are young.

Do not spend everything you earn. This sounds obvious, but it is where most people fail. The moment money comes in, they find a way to send it right back out. Learn to set something aside — even if it is small — before you spend anything else.

Avoid debt like it is a trap — because it is. "The borrower is servant to the lender" (Proverbs 22:7). Debt promises freedom and delivers bondage. There may come a time when some borrowing is necessary, but a young woman who learns to live within her means will save herself decades of financial stress.

Give first, save second, spend last. Most people reverse this order. They spend first, save if anything is left over, and give from the scraps. Flip it. When giving comes first, it sets the order of your heart — it reminds you that everything you have belongs to God, and you are managing it on His behalf.

Do not let money determine your worth. You are not more valuable because you have more. You are not less valuable because you have less. Your worth was settled at the cross, and no bank account can add to it or subtract from it.

> *Give first. Save second. Spend last.*

> *Money will test your character.*

It will reveal what you love, what you trust, and who you really are.

Let it find you faithful.

Where your treasure is, there your heart will be also.

For Further Study

Money is one of the most discussed topics in all of Scripture. These passages are a place to start.

- Matthew 6:19–21 — Where your treasure is

- 1 Timothy 6:6–10 — The love of money

- Luke 8:1–3 — Women who supported Jesus from their private means

- Acts 16:14–15, 40 — Lydia's generosity and hospitality

- Mark 12:41–44 — The widow's two coins

- Philippians 4:11–13 — The secret of contentment

- 2 Corinthians 9:6–7 — God loves a cheerful giver

- Hebrews 13:5 — Content with what you have

- Proverbs 22:7 — The borrower is servant to the lender

"Do not store up for yourselves treasures on earth, where moth and rust destroy, and where thieves break in and steal. But store up for yourselves treasures in heaven, where neither moth nor rust destroys, and where thieves do not break in or steal; for where your treasure is, there your heart will be also."

— Matthew 6:19–21 (NASB)

CHAPTER 14

The Church Is Not Optional

Part Four: How You Build a Life

You will hear people say it. You may have already said it yourself.

"I love God, but I do not need the church."

"I can worship God anywhere — on a mountain, on a beach, in my room."

"The church is full of hypocrites. I would rather follow Jesus on my own."

It sounds reasonable. It sounds mature, even — like you have outgrown the institution and arrived at something more authentic. The culture around you will applaud it. Plenty of people your age and older have adopted this exact position, and they will tell you they are happier for it.

But there is a problem. The Bible does not give you that option.

Not because the church is perfect. It is not. Not because every congregation gets everything right. They do not. But because the church is not a human invention that you can take or leave based on your preferences. It is God's design. He created it. Christ died for it. The Holy Spirit empowered it. And the New Testament makes no provision for a Christian who lives the faith alone.

*"They were continually devoting themselves to the apostles'
teaching and to fellowship, to the breaking of bread and to
prayer."*

— Acts 2:42 (NASB)

That is the first description of the church after it was established on
the day of Pentecost. About three thousand souls were added that
day (Acts 2:41), and this is what they did: they devoted themselves.
Not casually attended. Not occasionally dropped in. They devoted
themselves — to the teaching, to fellowship, to the breaking of
bread, and to prayer. Together.

> *The Christian faith was never designed to be practiced
> alone.*

What the Church Actually Is

Part of the confusion comes from how the word "church" is used
today. When most people hear it, they think of a building — a place
you drive to on Sunday morning. Stained glass, pews, a parking lot.
But that is not what the New Testament means by the word.

The Greek word is *ekklesia.* It means "the called out" — an
assembly of people called together for a purpose. In the New
Testament, it never refers to a building. It always refers to people.

When Paul wrote his letters, he did not write to buildings. He
wrote to "the church of God which is at Corinth" (1 Corinthians
1:2) — the people of God who assembled together in that city.
When he greeted Priscilla and Aquila, he greeted "the church that is

in their house" (Romans 16:5). The church met in homes, not cathedrals. It was not an institution first. It was a family.

Paul uses one image more than any other to describe the church: a body.

> *"For even as the body is one and yet has many members, and all the members of the body, though they are many, are one body, so also is Christ. For by one Spirit we were all baptized into one body."*
>
> — 1 Corinthians 12:12–13 (NASB)

You are not the whole body. You are a member — a part. An eye cannot say to the hand, "I have no need of you." A head cannot say to the feet, "I do not need you" (1 Corinthians 12:21). Every part needs the other parts. That is how the body works.

When you say "I do not need the church," you are saying "I do not need the body." And Paul says that is not how God designed it.

> *The church is not a building you attend. It is a body you belong to.*

The Command You Cannot Ignore

If the body metaphor is not enough, the writer of Hebrews makes it a direct command:

Do not forsake the assembling together. That is not a suggestion. It is a command — and the writer adds that some were already making a habit of neglecting it. This is not a new problem. People have been finding reasons to skip the assembly since the first century.

But notice what the assembly is for. It is not just about you getting something out of it — though you will. It is about stimulating one another to love and good deeds. It is about encouraging one another. The assembly exists so that Christians can build each other up. When you remove yourself from it, you are not only depriving yourself. You are depriving the body of what you were meant to contribute.

You need the church. And the church needs you.

> *You were not just invited to the assembly. You were commanded not to forsake it.*

Christ and the Church

If you are tempted to think the church does not matter much, consider how Christ thinks of it.

Christ loved the church. Not tolerated it. Not occasionally showed up for it. He loved it — and He died for it. He gave Himself up for her. The church is not an afterthought in God's plan. It is central to it. It is the bride of Christ — purchased with His blood.

When you treat the church as optional, you are treating as disposable something that Christ considered worth dying for. That should give you pause.

This does not mean the church is above criticism. It does not mean every congregation is healthy. It does not mean you should stay in a place that teaches error or harms people. But it does mean that the idea of the church — the assembly of God's people, gathering in His name, devoted to His word and to one another — is something God takes seriously. And He expects you to take it seriously too.

> *Christ loved the church enough to die for it. You can love it enough to show up.*

Women in the Early Church

The early church was full of women who gave themselves to the work.

You have already met Lydia — the seller of purple fabrics who opened her home to the church at Philippi (Acts 16:40). But she was not alone. When Paul wrote his letter to the church at Rome, he filled the final chapter with greetings to specific people. And many of them were women.

Consider Phoebe:

— Romans 16:1–2 (NASB)

Paul calls Phoebe a servant of the church — the Greek word is *diakonon,* which simply means "one who serves." It is used broadly throughout the New Testament of anyone who serves — Paul uses it of himself and of Christ. Phoebe was a woman who served the church, and served well. She helped many. She helped Paul himself. And Paul trusted her enough to commend her to the entire church at Rome. Many believe she was the one who carried Paul's letter to the Romans — one of the most important documents in Christian history — from Corinth to Rome.

Then there is Priscilla. Along with her husband Aquila, she was one of Paul's closest fellow workers. They met Paul in Corinth, where they worked together as tentmakers (Acts 18:1–3). They traveled with him. They risked their own necks for his life (Romans 16:3–4). And when a gifted preacher named Apollos came to Ephesus teaching accurately about Jesus but with an incomplete understanding, it was Priscilla and Aquila who "took him aside and explained to him the way of God more accurately" (Acts 18:26, NASB).

Paul greets them in Romans:

A church met in their home. They risked their lives for the gospel. Paul called them fellow workers. And all the churches of the Gentiles gave thanks for them.

These women were not spectators. They were not sitting in the back waiting for someone to tell them what to do. They were serving, teaching, hosting, supporting, carrying letters, and building the church from the inside out.

The church needs women like that today. It needs you.

The New Testament does assign different roles to men and women in the church. Elders, deacons, and preachers are roles Scripture gives to qualified men — not because men are superior, but because God designed a headship structure for both the home and the church (1 Corinthians 11:3, 1 Timothy 2:11–12, 1 Timothy 3:1–13). But different roles do not mean different value. Men and women are equal in worth, equal in salvation (Galatians 3:28), and equally essential to the body of Christ.

Women like Phoebe, Priscilla, and Lydia served powerfully within God's design — they did not need a title to build the church. Their work speaks for itself. And that should encourage you: you do not need a position to make a difference. You need faithfulness, a willing heart, and the courage to show up.

What the Assembly Looked Like

So what did the early church actually do when they gathered?

Acts 2:42 gives us the summary: they devoted themselves to the apostles' teaching, to fellowship, to the breaking of bread, and to prayer.

The apostles' teaching is what we now have preserved in the New Testament. When the church assembled, the word of God was taught. This was not optional entertainment. It was the foundation of everything they did.

Fellowship — the Greek word *koinonia* — means sharing, partnership, communion. It is not just socializing. It is the deep connection that comes from sharing the same faith, the same Lord, the same mission. You cannot have *koinonia* by yourself. It requires the assembly.

The breaking of bread refers to the Lord's Supper — the memorial that Jesus instituted the night before His death (Luke 22:19–20). Paul describes the church at Troas gathering "on the first day of the week" to break bread (Acts 20:7). This was the pattern: the church assembled on the first day of the week, and they observed the Lord's Supper together.

And prayer. Not just private prayer — though that matters — but corporate prayer. Christians praying together, lifting their voices together, interceding for one another and for the world.

And singing. Paul told the Ephesians: "Speaking to one another in psalms and hymns and spiritual songs, singing and making melody with your heart to the Lord" (Ephesians 5:19, NASB). And to the Colossians: "Teaching and admonishing one another with psalms and hymns and spiritual songs, singing with thankfulness in your hearts to God" (Colossians 3:16, NASB). Notice where the melody is made — in the heart. The New Testament pattern for worship is the human voice lifted to God, not a performance to be watched. When the church sings together, every voice matters. Yours included.

And giving. Paul instructed the Corinthians: "On the first day of every week each one of you is to put aside and save, as he may prosper" (1 Corinthians 16:1–2, NASB). This is not tithing — tithing was part of the Law of Moses. New Testament giving is proportional and purposeful: as you have been prospered, and as you have purposed in your heart, "not grudgingly or under compulsion, for God loves a cheerful giver" (2 Corinthians 9:7, NASB). Giving is an act of worship, not a tax.

This is what the assembly is for. Not performance. Not entertainment. Not a building program. The teaching, the fellowship, the Lord's Supper, prayer, singing, and giving. When a church is devoted to these things, it is doing what God designed it to do.

> *The church gathers for the teaching, the fellowship, the*
> *bread, the prayer, the singing, and the giving.*
> *Everything else is secondary.*

"But the Church Hurt Me"

This has to be addressed, because it is real.

Some of you have been hurt by people in the church. Maybe a leader was hypocritical. Maybe you were judged, excluded, or treated unkindly. Maybe the church you grew up in was more about appearances than truth. Maybe someone who claimed to represent Christ did something that did not look anything like Him.

That pain is real. And it is not dismissed by anything in this chapter.

But here is the truth you need to hold onto: the church is made up of imperfect people. It always has been. The church at Corinth was a mess — divisions, lawsuits, immorality, disorder at the Lord's table. Paul spent two entire letters correcting them. The churches in Galatia were being led astray by false teaching. The church at Laodicea was lukewarm and self-satisfied (Revelation 3:14–17).

The New Testament never pretends the church is perfect. But it never tells you to leave, either. It tells you to help make it better.

If you have been hurt, take that pain seriously. Talk to someone you trust. Find a congregation that teaches the truth and practices it. But do not use the failure of some Christians as an excuse to abandon what Christ established. The church is not the problem. Sin is the problem. And sin will follow you whether you are inside the church or outside of it.

The answer to a bad church experience is not no church. It is the right church — a church that holds to the apostles' teaching, that practices genuine fellowship, that gathers faithfully, and that cares more about truth than tradition.

You Are Needed

One more thing, and this is personal.

The church needs you. Not a future, more mature, more polished version of you. You — right now, as you are, with whatever you have to offer.

You may be young. You may feel like you do not know enough. You may think you have nothing to contribute. That is not true. The body needs every part. A young woman who shows up faithfully, who serves willingly, who encourages others, who studies the word and grows in her faith — that young woman is building something that will outlast her.

Do not wait until you feel ready. You will never feel ready. Show up anyway. Sit under the teaching. Sing the songs. Take the bread. Pray with your brothers and sisters. Let them encourage you, and encourage them in return. Be present — not just physically, but with your whole heart.

The church is not a building. It is not an event. It is the body of Christ on earth — and you are part of it.

They devoted themselves.

For Further Study

The New Testament is, in many ways, a book about the church. These passages are essential.

- Acts 2:41–47 — The first church and its devotion
- Hebrews 10:24–25 — Do not forsake the assembling together
- Ephesians 5:25 — Christ loved the church and gave Himself for her
- 1 Corinthians 12:12–27 — The body and its members
- Romans 16:1–5 — Phoebe, Priscilla, and the church in their house
- Acts 18:1–3, 24–26 — Priscilla and Aquila
- Acts 20:7 — The first day of the week
- Ephesians 5:19, Colossians 3:16 — Singing and making melody in the heart
- 1 Corinthians 16:1–2, 2 Corinthians 9:6–7 — Giving as you have prospered

• Revelation 3:14–22 — The warning to the lukewarm
church

"They were continually devoting
themselves to the apostles' teaching and
to fellowship, to the breaking of bread
and to prayer."

— Acts 2:42 (NASB)

Your Move

We have covered a lot of ground together.

We talked about your name — and why it is the most valuable thing you own. We talked about the mirror — and why what God sees matters more than what you see. We talked about integrity — the person you are when nobody is watching. We talked about purpose — the fact that you were made on purpose, for a purpose.

We talked about the relationship you need most — and why it is not with a man, but with Jesus. We talked about the Bible — what it is, what it is not, and why it matters. We talked about stillness — and the discipline of putting down the noise long enough to hear something true.

We talked about how you treat the young men around you. We talked about the friends you choose and how they will shape your future. We talked about honoring your parents — even when it is hard. We talked about work, about money, and about the church.

And through all of it, one thing has been underneath everything:

> *"The fear of the LORD is the beginning of wisdom, and the knowledge of the Holy One is understanding."*
> — Proverbs 9:10 (NASB)

That is where we started. And that is where we end. Because everything in this book — every chapter, every principle, every piece of advice — means nothing if you do not have the foundation to build it on.

The foundation is not self-improvement. It is not good intentions. It is not trying harder. The foundation is God — knowing Him, fearing Him, and surrendering your life to Him through His Son, Jesus Christ.

> *Everything in this book stands or falls on this one question: what will you do with Jesus?*

The Problem You Cannot Fix

Here is the truth that every other chapter has been pointing toward.

You are a sinner.

That is not an insult. It is a diagnosis. And it applies to every person who has ever lived — except One.

> *"For all have sinned and fall short of the glory of God."*
> — Romans 3:23 (NASB)

All have sinned. Not some. Not the especially bad ones. All. You, me, the woman sitting next to you in class, the man preaching on Sunday morning. Every human being has fallen short of God's standard.

And the consequence of that sin is real:

> *"For the wages of sin is death."*
> — Romans 6:23a (NASB)

Sin pays wages, and those wages are death — not just physical death, but spiritual separation from God. That is the problem. It is not that you are imperfect and need to try harder. It is that you are separated from a holy God by your sin, and there is nothing you can do on your own to bridge that gap.

No amount of good behavior can erase what has already been done. No number of good deeds can outweigh the debt. You cannot fix this yourself. If you could, Christ would not have needed to come.

> *You cannot save yourself. That is not a weakness. That is the starting point.*

What God Did About It

But Romans 6:23 does not end there. Read the whole verse:

> *"For the wages of sin is death, but the free gift of God is eternal life in Christ Jesus our Lord."*
>
> — Romans 6:23 (NASB)

The wages of sin is death — but the gift of God is eternal life. It is a gift. Not earned. Not purchased. Not achieved through effort. Given freely by a God who loved you enough to pay the price Himself.

> *"But God demonstrates His own love toward us, in that while we were yet sinners, Christ died for us."*
>
> — Romans 5:8 (NASB)

While we were *yet sinners.* Not after we cleaned ourselves up. Not after we proved we were worthy. While we were still in the middle of it — while we were still lost, still broken, still separated from Him — Christ died for us.

Jesus, the Son of God, left heaven, put on human flesh, lived a perfect life that you and I could never live, and then went to a cross and bore the punishment that you and I deserved. He died in your place. He took your sin upon Himself so that you could be made right with God.

> *"He made Him who knew no sin to be sin on our behalf, so that we might become the righteousness of God in Him."*
> — 2 Corinthians 5:21 (NASB)

That is the gospel. That is the good news. Not that God is waiting for you to be good enough. Not that He will accept you once you have earned it. But that He has already done what you could not do — and He offers it to you as a gift.

> *The gospel is not about what you must do for God. It is about what God has already done for you.*

What He Asks of You

The gift is free. But it must be received. God will not force salvation on anyone. He offers it — and then He asks you to respond.

So what does He ask?

He asks you to **believe.** Not just to acknowledge that God exists — even the demons believe that (James 2:19). But to trust in Jesus as the Son of God, the risen Lord, the only way to the Father.

> *"I am the way, and the truth, and the life; no one comes to the Father but through Me."*
>
> — John 14:6 (NASB)

He asks you to **repent.** To turn away from sin and turn toward God. Repentance is not just feeling sorry — it is a change of mind that leads to a change of direction.

> *"Therefore repent and return, so that your sins may be wiped away, in order that times of refreshing may come from the presence of the Lord."*
>
> — Acts 3:19 (NASB)

He asks you to **confess.** To declare openly and without shame that Jesus Christ is Lord.

> *"If you confess with your mouth Jesus as Lord, and believe in your heart that God raised Him from the dead, you will be saved."*
>
> — Romans 10:9 (NASB)

And He asks you to be **baptized.** Not as an optional add-on. Not as a symbol that comes later when you feel ready. Baptism is the point at which you are united with Christ in His death, burial, and resurrection — it is where your sins are washed away.

"Repent, and each of you be baptized in the name of Jesus Christ for the forgiveness of your sins; and you will receive the gift of the Holy Spirit."

— Acts 2:38 (NASB)

"Or do you not know that all of us who have been baptized into Christ Jesus have been baptized into His death? Therefore we have been buried with Him through baptism into death, so that as Christ was raised from the dead through the glory of the Father, so we too might walk in newness of life."

— Romans 6:3–4 (NASB)

Believe. Repent. Confess. Be baptized. That is what the New Testament teaches. Not one step alone, but all of them — each one part of the response God asks of you.

> *The gift is free. But it must be received. And God has told you how.*

Choose This Day

Thousands of years ago, an old man stood before the nation of Israel and gave them a choice. Joshua had led the people into the promised land. He had fought the battles. He had seen God's faithfulness firsthand. And now, near the end of his life, he gathered the people and said:

"If it is disagreeable in your sight to serve the LORD, choose for yourselves today whom you will serve: whether the gods which your fathers served which were beyond the River, or the gods of the Amorites in whose land you are living; but as for me and my house, we will serve the LORD."

— Joshua 24:15 (NASB)

Choose for yourselves today.

Not tomorrow. Not when you feel ready. Not when life settles down. Not when you have it all figured out. Today. This is the day of decision. This is the moment you have been reading toward.

Joshua did not wait for the crowd to make up its mind before he made his own decision. He declared it: *as for me and my house, we will serve the LORD.* He was not asking for consensus. He was making a commitment — publicly, clearly, and without apology.

That is what this book has been building toward. Not information. Not inspiration. A decision.

> *Choose for yourselves today.*

Your Move

You have heard the truth. Not every truth — no book can give you that. But enough truth to know what matters, where to look for more, and what God is asking of you.

You know that your name matters and that your character is being built right now, in the choices nobody sees. You know that the relationship you need most is with Jesus, that the Bible is the word of God, and that stillness is where you learn to hear His voice. You know how to treat people — young men, friends, parents — with the honor and wisdom God requires. You know that your work and your money reveal what you really love. And you know that the church is not optional — it is where God's people gather, and it is where you belong.

But knowing is not enough. James said it plainly:

> *"But prove yourselves doers of the word, and not merely hearers who delude themselves."*
>
> — James 1:22 (NASB)

You can read this entire book, agree with every word, and close it unchanged. That is a real possibility. Knowledge without action is just information. And information that does not change your life is the most dangerous kind — because it gives you the illusion of growth while you stand perfectly still.

Do not be that woman.

Be the woman who hears the word and does it. Be the woman who builds her house on the rock and not on sand (Matthew 7:24–27). Be the woman who fears God, who works with her hands in delight, who clothes herself in strength and dignity and smiles at the future.

Be the woman who, when it was her turn to choose, chose well.

This is your move.

Nobody can make it for you. Nobody can make it instead of you.

As for me and my house, we will serve the LORD.

> *"Strength and dignity are her clothing, and she smiles at the future."*
>
> — Proverbs 31:25 (NASB)